CASH POOR
or COL

THE ESSENTIAL GUIDE TO COLLEGE ADMISSIONS

FOR

TEENS (AGES 13 TO 18) & THEIR PARENTS

by Diane M. Warmsley

MOtivational PRESS®
LEADERS IN GLOBAL PUBLISHING

To Bria,
Diane M. Warmsley

Published by Motivational Press, Inc.
7777 N Wickham Rd, # 12-247
Melbourne, FL 32940
www.MotivationalPress.com

Manufactured in the United States of America.

ISBN: 978-1-62865-123-2

Contents

Dedication

This book is dedicated to the memory of my mother, Gladys C. Booker, who instilled the value of education and worked tirelessly to make my successful completion of college possible.

Foreword

I was delighted when I received a request from Diane Warmsley to write a brief foreword to this book. I was immediately transported back to the days when both she and I were standing behind tables, representing our respective colleges, to deliver a message to prospective students. These were the days of cutting our teeth on college admission counseling.

During these years, I found Diane to be passionate about guiding students. I was most impressed however, by her desire and thirst for knowledge particularly as it related to improving the college preparation experiences for underrepresented students in the United States. Her untiring devotion to research and study about our profession moved me to recommend her for participation in a respected Summer Institute sponsored by the National Association of College Admissions Counselors (NACAC). And she successfully landed a year-long Research Scholar opportunity with NACAC after a national search for proposals. Fast forward to 2005, I was not surprised to learn that she nailed the top admissions job at York College/CUNY. She had built up a significant track record in the admissions world as a recruiter, counselor, administrator, and researcher.

Cash Poor or College? represents Diane's sincere commitment to see continued growth in the pipeline of teens moving on to college. Her work is infused with well-researched information, time-tested lessons and practical tools. What stands out most for me about this book is:

▶ *the emphasis placed on preparation from high school start to finish*

▶ *the mix of information and practical tools to support teen development*

▶ *the direct and digestible messaging*

▶ *the concrete ways parents can support their teen in the journey towards college*

Cash Poor or College? is sorely needed now when families, educators and interested stakeholders are concerned about preparing adolescents for the world beyond high school – the world of tomorrow.

Dr Fay Maureen Butler
Pastor, Consultant, Business Owner
Author of *Breadcrumbs. Vol 1-* Inspirational
Thoughts and Motivational Quotes

Acknowledgments

I wish to acknowledge those who generously gave permission for use of their content including Shanda Ivory, NACAC, The Pell Institute for the Study of Opportunity in Higher Education, Lynn O'Shaughnessy (The CollegeSolution.com), Leo Widrich (Lifehacker.com), Rahul Chowdhury (Hongkiat. com), and John Baker (Desire2Learn.com). A very special thanks to my husband, Raymond Warmsley, for the enormity of his support; to my children for allowing me to experiment new ways to inspire their learning; to Dr. Fay Maureen Butler, author of *Breadcrumbs*, for her generous sharing of resources that expedited the publishing of this book; to Justin Sachs, President of Motivational Press, for seeing the merits of this work and choosing it for publication; to Leslie Jay, copy editor; to Steve Asfall of The Creative Flow, graphic designer for the book cover; and to the countless students who gave me the opportunity to provide higher education counsel, throughout my career.

To the Student

Dear Student,

You are probably wondering why this book is titled *Cash Poor or College*. Frankly, it was inspired by a recent wave of strikes at fast-food restaurants, all across the nation. Employees working at these establishments know all too well that they are not making a "living wage," a wage that keeps them (and their families) out of poverty. This movement also makes clear that people lacking competitive skills are absolutely more likely to be situated in low-paying jobs. You don't have to wind up in this dead-end trap. There is another road that you can travel and that is the purpose of this book.

Cash Poor or College? The Essential Guide to College Admissions for Teens & Their Parents lays out a path that you can follow to ensure that you do not enter the job market on its lowest rung. Instead, this book seeks to position you to assume a career that spirals ever upward. Your future begins with your high school journey and how well you utilize it to your best advantage.

The Guide's main target is YOU. I have no doubt that from the point you enter high school, you can be *primarily* responsible for your educational outcomes. I also believe that if you are armed with the right kinds of information, provided at the right points in your high school career, you can make informed decisions about your post-high school educational pursuits.

Here are specific ways that this Guide will assist you in this process:

1. It *breaks down the high school experience, year by year,* so that you know exactly what information to digest and tasks to accomplish.

2. It *provides detailed information to help you to make knowledgeable decisions* about your academic preparation in high school.

3. It *presents practical assignments* that ready you for the college admission process.

4. It *outlines the college admission process* in detail.

5. It *furnishes forms and checklists* to help you organize activities and track your progress and results.

In closing, I hope you will employ the information and tools that are laid out for you in *Cash Poor or College?* so that you can fast-track your way to the college of your dreams!

To Your Success,

Diane M. Warmsley

Message to the Professional Community

Ibegan working on *Cash Poor or College? The Essential Guide to College Admissions for Teens & Their Parents* in 2004, but put it on hold when I became Director of Admissions at a public, four-year institution. I returned to the project because recent conversations with high school students led me to conclude that such a Guide was essential, now more than ever.

What happened? The game changed for countless students in 2008, when the bottom dropped out of the economy. A confluence of circumstances undermined the college prospects for many students. High schools became increasingly challenged to stretch resources, resulting in much heavier student loads per counselor. All too many students experienced difficulty getting face-time with counselors and, when they did, the encounter was rushed. As a result, fewer students today are able to access vital information that would help them make knowledgeable decisions about their pathway to college. Even schools that once had robust college prep offerings have reduced, if not scrapped, initiatives in the wake of requisite budget cuts.

Concurrently, families have had to make adjustments to household budgets due to job loss and/or lower-paying job assignments. Low-income families, who have traditionally counted on educational opportunity programs to assist with college costs, are finding that fewer slots are now available. Middle-income families, too, are increasingly faced with the harsh realities of reducing expenses and reigning in family debt, while college tuitions continue to rise in every sector – public and private.

Further, and this has long been the case, discussion about college admission gets under way much too late in students' high school careers. In all too many places, students do not begin gearing up for college until the spring of the junior year, at best, or fall of the senior year, at worst – much too late to influence academic preparation that could markedly improve college admission outcomes.

Given the compelling circumstances described above, *Cash Poor or College?* was reborn in hopes of offering high school students a strategic approach to accessing higher education. First, the high school student is positioned as the prime target to actualize a college admissions plan. While parents and professionals are expected to provide ample support to students, it is this author's view that armed with the right kinds of information, provided at the right points in the high school experience, students can be successful in navigating their personal journey.

Second, the Guide introduces a "college admission pipeline model" that utilizes the entire high school experience as a platform for scaffolding information to the student. From the point of middle school graduation to high school completion, the Guide exposes students to an array of data, resource listings, and advisories to inspire progress.

Lastly, the Guide aims to be informative, if not exhaustive. It is meant to supplement other materials and programming that address discrete aspects of college search in much greater detail.

As a parent, admissions counselor and minority student recruiter, senior administrator of an educational opportunity program, college scholarship developer, higher education researcher, and former Director of Admissions who has helped countless high schoolers navigate their way to college, I have infused this work with practical information and personal insights gleaned over twenty-five years. I sincerely hope that you find *Cash Poor or College?* valuable as an additional tool in helping students prepare for their journey toward college.

How to Use this Guide

» **The *Cash Poor or College? Guide* should not be read all at once. *Whew!*** Instead, it's designed to present information as you need it. So, you should read all the material before and including the year you are about to enter. For example, *before* entering freshman year, you should read the sections "Is College in Your Future?" and "Freshmen" (see Table of Contents). During the summer *after* freshman year, you should read the section for "Sophomores."

» The Guide presents only the information *most essential* to your understanding of college preparation principles and college admission planning. This allows you to focus on absorbing the suggestions and employing the activities that help move you forward.

» The word "college" is used throughout this book to refer to any *educational* venture that follows high school completion. This could include certificate programs, as well as degree programs.

» Gems of information are sprinkled throughout the book and appear in captions as follows:

- *factual* tidbits

HMMMM - ideas that create a deeper connection to a topic

TIP - tips and suggestions for activities

» You will notice that the vocabulary gets more powerful as you move through the book. This is intended to mirror the increased word development that should be taking place as you move through your upper grades in high school.

» The Guide should be viewed as a supplement to all conversations and activities that take place in your high school. It should lead you to check out college resources that address specific topics, such as financial aid, scholarships, essay writing, and so on.

» The **Appendices** consist of important items, including "College Search Websites," the "A, B, C's of College Terms," and assorted Forms to help you organize and track college-search activities.

IS COLLEGE IN

YOUR FUTURE?

Why College Matters

So, why bother go to college? Depending on who you ask, answers to this question will vary. But, I bet the following reasons would top the list:

1) Money (productive employment)

2) Money and security (personal earnings over a lifetime)

3) Money, security and personal fulfillment (prepares you for the future)

PRODUCTIVE EMPLOYMENT

One day soon, you will be expected to make your way in this world, without the assistance of your parents or other adults. To fend for yourself financially, you will likely choose one of the following paths:

1) Go to work after high school graduation

2) Enter the military, or

3) Continue your education

You certainly can be productive through one of the first two options, but these choices have certain consequences. Entering the world of work right after high school will keep your income low for some years to come. And entering the military carries a real life-and-death risk. On the other hand, choosing to continue your education can prepare you for opportunities long into the future and raise your lifetime earnings.

Let's see how this works! Take a good look at the chart in *figure 1*. It shows that even during a period of deep economic recession, earnings were higher for those who completed more education. Find "high school grads" whose yearly income was $58,809 (2010). Now, find "associate's degrees" income of $77,098, and "bachelor's degrees" at $108,402. *What this means is that folks with college degrees made $49,593 more a year than those with high school diplomas!*

Figure 1. Average family income by educational level in 2010.
Courtesy of The Pell Institute for the Study of Opportunity in Higher Education, Postsecondary Education Opportunity, www.postsecondary.org.

Here is another way to look at income. Let's consider the effect of an economic recession, like the one we have been in since 2008. Many people with and without college degrees have lost their jobs.

The chart in *figure 2* shows how closely unemployment is tied to earnings. Let's start at the bottom of the chart and focus on the numbers on the left. As your eyes rise to the top, you notice that the numbers get lower and lower. This demonstrates that *individuals with more education were less likely to be unemployed* in 2012.

Now, focus on the right side of the chart and start at the top. As your eyes move down, you notice that the income drops with the educational level. This shows *that the more education people had, the higher their incomes were* in 2011.

A final point of information made clear by this chart is that *those who complete even some college have an increased chance of being employed and earning more than those with just a high school diploma.*

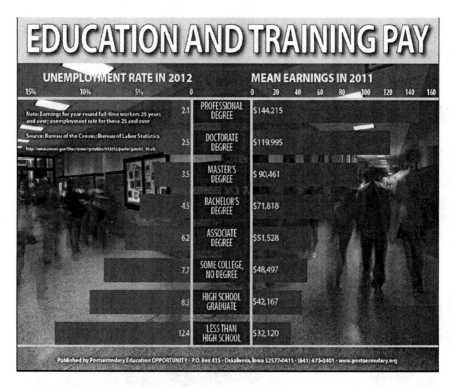

Figure 2. The unemployment rate in 2012 by education level and the mean earnings in 2011 by education level. Courtesy of The Pell Institute for the Study of Opportunity in Higher Education, Postsecondary Education Opportunity, www.postsecondary.org.

PERSONAL LIFE-TIME EARNINGS

It is a fact that the more education a person has, the more he or she is likely to earn over the course of a lifetime. The chart in *figure 3* shows that over 40 years or so, employees' lifetime earnings get much higher as their education level increases. Again, let's find "high school graduates" who made a total of *$863,000* for about 40 years of work. Now, compare this figure with "associate's degree" holders who made *$1,303,000*, over the same amount of time. Last, find "bachelor's degree" holders who made $1,711,000. **Wow!** *College grads earned $848,000 more than high school grads over their entire working years – almost double the income!*

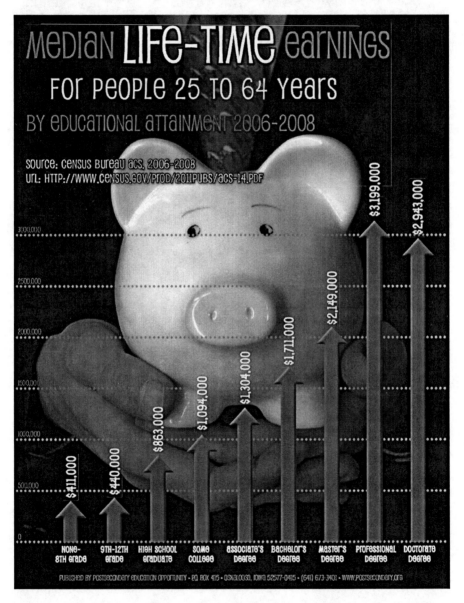

Figure 3. The median lifetime earnings for people by education level, 2006-2008. Courtesy of The Pell Institute for the Study of Opportunity in Higher Education, *Postsecondary Education Opportunity*, www.postsecondary.org.

PREPARATION FOR THE FUTURE

In recent years, employers have stated that America is not producing enough qualified candidates for many jobs. *How is this possible?* Well, it seems that 1) the current education model is proving inadequate to prepare workers for today's employment demands, 2) jobs are being moved overseas in search of more qualified workers, and 3) America's youth continues to slip in competitiveness behind China, South Korea and Japan.

What do you need to know? A new era, the **Knowledge Economy,** is dawning, fueled by rapid advances in communications and technology. It is reshaping our world at an extraordinary pace. Just think how quickly cell phone technology has turned over in recent years. "No one could have imagined that in a mere 17 years, mobile phones could have made the leap ... to becoming a computer, GPS, radio and our lifeline to the Internet, and still be able to fit in your pocket."[1] Advances in other arenas - transportation, health care, communications, medicine, the military, space and consumer products – demand a skilled workforce now and for the foreseeable future. High school diplomas alone just won't cut it.

What do employers want? An employer puts it this way:

"What I need most of all are employees who can take solution A and solution B and figure out how to come up with a new solution, C. People like that are rare.

They have to understand the problems, analyze the bigger picture, predict the ramifications of what they are proposing, synthesize new knowledge, be creative as they problem solve and collaborate."[2]

What can be done? Until the majority of American high schools create programs that prepare students for the new economy, it will be necessary to seek advanced learning in post-high school experiences. So, if you truly want to prepare for future employment, then continuing your education should be priority No. 1.

I hope that you are now convinced to give college a try. If so, read on to learn how to prepare to connect to the best colleges available.

Marie's Story: True Admissions Tale

Now, let's meet Marie[*]. She is a young lady who has been successful in attaining a college education, master's degree and doctoral degree (in progress) without going into debt! How did she do it? Here is her story in a nutshell...

BACKGROUND

At 15, Marie reached out for help to identify a range of colleges to explore. She was in her sophomore year of high school and came from a middle-income household in New York State. She had grades in the 90's (except for physical education) and had completed a strong college preparatory program. A solid student across the board, she was still not ready to name a college major. And she wasn't sure whether to go away to school or stay home, or whether to live in a dorm or attend a commuter college.

THE COLLEGE SEARCH PLAN

The plan devised for Marie's junior year included the following activities:

▶ *Look at colleges/universities with strong liberal arts programs*

▶ *Visit colleges in the mid-Atlantic and northeastern region of the country*

▶ *Investigate public and private institutions, ranked as selective*

▶ *Inquire about scholarships*

▶ *Pick one Ivy institution to explore*

When Marie's senior year SAT scores tipped the 1300[**] mark, she was further advised to inquire about a relatively new phenomenon known as Honors Colleges.

During the application season, eight institutions were identified as being excellent prospects for Marie; two had Honors Colleges and one had a highly regarded math and science program.

THE RESULTS

Marie gained admission to seven of her eight choices, including the math/science program and both Honors College choices. She did not prevail with the Ivy choice presumably because she had not "demonstrated interest" prior to submitting an application (i.e. attendance at campus tours or open houses, contact with admissions representatives, etc.). This was deemed an important factor in qualifying students for admission the year that Marie applied.

In the end, Marie chose to attend CUNY Honors College– know known as the Macauley Honors College, available at eight participating campuses in the City University of New York. There were many benefits to this selection, including a high-caliber liberal arts education, full-tuition abatement, free dormitory facilities, a sizeable study abroad stipend, and many other perks. ***The bottom line was that Marie would go to college WITHOUT BORROWING MONEY!***

I share Marie's story to illustrate what can happen for YOU! At the heart of this story is the fact that Marie prepared herself to compete and, in turn, was rewarded with great offers of admission. You, too, can create a pathway to success by trusting this Guide to help you blaze that trail.

WHAT'S MARIE DOING NOW?

Marie decided to complete a BA/MA in mathematics, a major she found her way to in college. She participated in two study abroad programs, in South Africa and Argentina. Now she is pursuing a doctorate in Applied Mathematics at Cornell, an Ivy institution that eluded her at the undergraduate level.

---

*Marie is a fictitious name used to protect the true identity of the student; all other facts are true.

**1300 score comprised Critical Reading and Mathematics only (prior to SAT re-structuring in 2005).

What You Must Bring To The Party!

Marie's story makes clear that she was willing to take charge of her destiny. She made decisions to attend classes, study hard, and strive for success. If you, too, can embrace the belief that YOU are responsible for your educational outcomes, you will be off to a great start.

What you must bring to the party, then, are winning strategies that will ensure success throughout your high school journey. Using this catchy expression is a way of calling attention to **7 Winning Values** that, if practiced routinely, can set you up for amazing transformation and accomplishment.

1. Embody a Formula for Success

You probably have heard the expression "if you can believe it, you can achieve it." Let's look more closely at the meaning behind this statement. The phrase "believe it" suggests the taking hold of an idea. Perhaps you *believe* that one day you will be an engineer. Having this idea is wonderful, but it is just the first step. It is not until you take *action* to move in the direction of the goal that the idea has a chance of coming into reality.

For example, when you believe that you will become an engineer and take steps to improve your math skills, attend engineering forums, and speak with practicing engineers, you are   taking action to *achieve* your goal. So, the next time you hear "if you can believe it, you can achieve it," visualize this simple formula:

BELIEF + ACTION = ACHIEVEMENT

2. TRANSCEND ANTI-ACADEMIC MESSAGING

Sadly, an "anti-academic" and "anti-smart" sentiment has seeped into youth culture in recent years. It has done more to undermine the potential of young folks than possibly anything else I can identify. It has created an environment of underachievement for way too many students, who could otherwise qualify for outstanding opportunities.

For sure, if you want successful outcomes, you have to be willing to stand above this tide, difficult though it may be. It will take courage, but just imagine if President Barack Obama, First Lady Michelle (Robinson) Obama, Associate Justice of the Supreme Court Sonia Sotomayor, media mogul Oprah Winfrey, former senator Daniel Inouye, and politicians Julian and Joaquin Castro (just to name a few) had given in to such pressure. We all would have lost out on the mighty contribution of their gifts and talents to the nation at large.

3. Commit to High Achievement

Over my career, the question students most often asked was, "What kind of grades do I need to get in to college?" My response would go something like this...

A very close relative is in need of heart surgery. You must select a cardiologist to perform the operation. If you could see the doctors' academic records from medical school, do you pick the one with a 75, 85 or 95 average?

<u>or</u>

Your car needs new brakes and you learn that the mechanic barely passed the course on brake work. Will you feel safe entrusting your job to him?

Do you get the point? Professionals looking to employ you or admit you to college know your value by the attention you've paid to your educational development. Grades are the most obvious indicator of the work you have put in and the value you have invested in yourself. It is wise to remember that before you can expect the world to take you seriously, you must *first* take yourself seriously!

So, the answer to the question above is: "You need the very best grades that you can earn."

HMMM

WHEN YOU ENTER A NEW CLASS, YOU BEGIN WITH A GRADE OF 100! YOUR GOAL IS TO STAY CLOSE TO THIS MARK FOR THE REST OF THE TERM!

4. SHOW UP

School is your training ground, just as the runner uses the track field, the ballerina uses the studio and the boxer uses the ring. These places are where they, and YOU, practice to perform at ever better heights. One of the most valuable behaviors that you should practice is "showing up." This means that getting to school *on time* and *regularly* is imperative. The more time you spend in the classroom, the more information you will be exposed to. And when you translate this behavior to other settings, you just never know whom you may meet or what vital piece of information you may hear.

"80 PERCENT OF SUCCESS IS SHOWING UP."

– WOODY ALLEN

5. AVOID EXCUSE-MAKING

One of the most self-defeating behaviors to be aware of is excuse-making. This is when someone tries to explain why something didn't happen, but should have. The problem with excuse-making is that it clouds your ability to learn from the outcome of events, both good and bad. So that you don't miss out on valuable lessons, it is a much better practice to look for reasons why situations occurred in the way that they did. This posture allows you to acknowledge "the good" so that it can be repeated, and note "the errors" so that they can be identified and avoided in the future.

6. Get Work Done First

Life is about balance. We benefit from work as much as play and we need both. The challenge is to fit both activities into our lives, in a balanced and orderly way. We have the best chance at success when we commit to doing *work first* and engaging in social activities afterwards. This practice ensures that your work is accomplished and submitted on time. You will appreciate the benefit of arranging your activities in this way as there is nothing scarier than waiting until the last minute to complete an assignment, seeing all that has to be done, and realizing that you have run out of time.

7. Dial Down Criticism

As you grow into a fuller understanding of the goals you want to achieve and the values you hold dear, you will want to be on the lookout for those who don't share your aspirations and dreams. These persons show up as naysayers, often lobbing put-downs or criticisms in your direction. Anyone in your world, even family members, can be guilty, so you want to "dial down" these voices wherever they appear.

Instead, seek to "tune up" the voices of those who have your best interests at heart and provide positive feedback and support. True friends will fall into this category, so keep them very close.

"SURROUND YOURSELF
WITH THE DREAMERS AND THE DOERS,
THE BELIEVERS AND THINKERS,
BUT MOST OF ALL,
SURROUND YOURSELF
WITH THOSE WHO SEE GREATNESS WITHIN YOU,
EVEN WHEN YOU DON'T SEE IT YOURSELF."

– EDMOND LEE

8. REVIEW 7 WINNING VALUES

How does anyone become good at anything? *They practice!* Whether it is learning how to play an instrument or perfecting a technique to improve your long jump, practice is necessary. So it is with the discipline required to secure strong academic behaviors. For this reason, it is recommended that you review these seven winning strategies at the beginning of each high school term, to ensure that you are working them into your everyday life.

"WATCH YOUR THOUGHTS;

    THEY BECOME WORDS.

WATCH YOUR WORDS;

    THEY BECOME ACTIONS.

WATCH YOUR ACTIONS;

    THEY BECOME HABITS.

WATCH YOUR HABITS;

    THEY BECOME CHARACTER.

WATCH YOUR CHARACTER;

    IT BECOMES YOUR DESTINY!"

             – LAO TZE

Before you read any further, consider the following scenario:

It's September of your senior year. You know you will be applying to colleges soon and fantasize about the day a letter of acceptance to the college of your dreams arrives.

Before this can happen, however, you've got to get a lot done. Each month, you need to complete a series of tasks along with your normal school and home obligations.

What are these tasks? The big ticket items are just about all of the following:

- *visitations to colleges*
- *completion of freshman applications*
- *completion of scholarship applications*
- *securing letters of recommendation*
- *taking standardized tests*
- *submitting financial aid application(s)*
- *interviewing*
- *interpreting financial aid response letters*

- ▶ *attending freshman programming*
- ▶ *making a final college selection*
- ▶ *attending pre-freshman programming*
- ▶ *meeting deadlines, throughout*

Sound overwhelming? Well, it needn't take your breath away. But, to accomplish it all, you will need to have a *serious and focused* plan. That plan is laid out for you in this Guide and you can begin the preparation, starting now. *Read on!*

FRESHMEN

(9th Grade)

Lay the Foundation

Must-know Tips for 9th Grade

Contrary to popular opinion, preparing for college does not begin in the junior or senior year of high school. In truth, the moment you enter high school, the game is on! Your freshman year is all about laying a solid foundation for success. You want to focus on strengthening your reading, writing, time management and study skills. Mastering these skills early on will serve you well when school work gets more challenging in the upper grades.

▶ *Get off to a Great Start*

At the outset, it is important to know just what you will be working to accomplish over the next few years. The goal will be to complete a college preparatory curriculum, so that *by the end of junior year*, you have undertaken the following academic program in high school:

3 years of English

3 years of Mathematics (Algebra, Geometry, Trigonometry, Precalculus, Calculus)

3 years of Science (Biology, Chemistry, Physics, Earth/ Space Science)

2-3 years of Social Studies

2-3 years of Foreign Language

1 year of performing or visual arts

▶ *Commit to Excellence*

Committing to excellence means having the willingness to test one's full potential. All too many students settle for mediocre results *before* they have exhausted their capabilities. This, in turn, makes them shy away from taking on new challenges. Instead, strive to achieve your *personal best*. You won't break and it doesn't hurt at all. In fact, it feels exhilarating and empowering!

> *HMMM*
>
> *IMAGINE YOURSELF RECEIVING HONORS, AWARDS, SCHOLARSHIPS AND/OR BEING INDUCTED INTO YOUR HIGH SCHOOL'S HONOR SOCIETY. CONSIDER THE PRIDE YOUR FAMILY WILL FEEL WHEN APPLAUDING YOUR ACCOMPLISHMENTS.*

▶ *Get Busy*

Your active involvement in high school allows you to discover and ex-

Did You Know?

Just about every scholarship and college application asks students to identify their participation in "extracurricular activities".
Be sure to have something to include.

plore your gifts and talents, develop people skills and get you noticed by teachers and counselors. So, join a club, athletic program, theater group and/or volunteer time to work in a high school office. You may even want to seek positions of leadership in student government and other youth groups. Continue to stay involved in your church and community. This will signal to colleges and scholarship donors that you are responsible and up for a challenge.

▶ *Friends as Support Agents*

When you enter high school, you have an opportunity to make new friends. Look to broaden your friendship circle to include those who have a positive outlook on life and toward school.

Striving for success is challenging and made so much easier when you are in the company of others who support your efforts — who better to understand than those on the same journey? You don't have to give up old friends; just balance out your relationships. At the end of the day, however, *remember that friends should lift you up!*

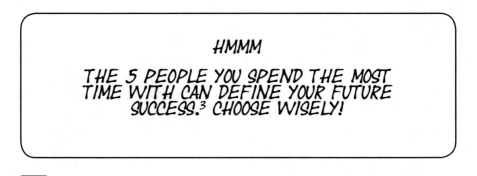

HMMM

THE 5 PEOPLE YOU SPEND THE MOST TIME WITH CAN DEFINE YOUR FUTURE SUCCESS.[3] CHOOSE WISELY!

▶ *Build Your College Fund*

Attending college is an expensive proposition no matter where you decide to go. To get ready for this expense, you should begin to build your college fund, now. First, start a savings account with a local bank (if you don't already have one). Next, begin making contributions to this account from cash gifts, money earned from work, and money you get from scholarships. Just so you know, there are oodles of scholarships to tap online and at various institutions, such as banks, community organizations, workplaces, city and state governments, churches, etc. A select Scholarship Resource List is provided on p. 114 to let you see the range of available offerings.

Be creative in your online scholarship searches to include your academic interest, athletic ability, artistic talents, and/or financial need. For example, see what comes up when you search "scholarships for left-handed people" or "first in the family to attend college scholarships." *Think outside the box!*

▶ *Teacher Connections*

Teachers can be your best resource for general information, recommendations on colleges, and specific subject area knowledge. They have all been to college and may have sent their children or grandchildren, as well. Their feedback can be valuable. So, you will want to establish good relations with your teachers, as you never know when you may need a bit of information, wise counsel or letter of recommendation.

▶ Practice "Code-Switching"

We all use *casual language* when we are speaking with our family and friends. It's relaxed and doesn't have any real rules. This is the same for the way we dress and how we behave.

But when we enter the world of school or work, the expectations change. When we encounter teachers, counselors and employers, we are expected to demonstrate mastery of Standard English, exhibit appropriate attire and temperate behavior. Having the ability to move easily between these two worlds — the casual and the professional—is a process called "code switching." It's not hard to do; it just requires practice. Just think of all the people who can speak two or more languages. They have learned how to code-switch in precisely the same manner.

TIP

To improve your language skills, continue to develop and increase your vocabulary. With friends who are willing, challenge each other to use new words in one-to-one communications. You will not only be improving your written and oral language skills, you will also be preparing for the SAT. New words can be drawn from a list at www.freevocabulary.com. *Try this; it can be fun!*

▶ The Power of Language

Have you taken classes in a foreign language and wondered what its value is? The answer to this question may rest on two important points:

1. Working to build proficiency in another language really improves your overall ability to learn.

2. Individuals who can speak and understand another language are highly valued in today's job market. As our country becomes more interconnected with other nations, the more people who can speak, write and communicate in other languages will be needed. Just think, having this additional skill could mean the difference in you getting a job over someone who is only monolingual. So, the next time you are sitting in a language class, you will want to take it very seriously.

If you have family members who speak another language, you have been given a gift! Take advantage of the opportunity to communicate with them in their primary language. This is, after all, your heritage and it does not take anything away from your American experience – *it adds to it!*

▶ *Summer Exploration*

Summer is surely a time for relaxation and fun. It can also be a time to increase your learning, while you enjoy yourself. Many summer programs and camps allow you to pick and choose academic topics of interest and/or explore the arts or athletics.

Another summer activity to consider is volunteering at a community organization or professional office. This is an excellent way to gain exposure to a career you may be considering. There is nothing like working in a hospital or doctor's office, if you are thinking about becoming a nurse, doctor or medical professional. Or, how about working at a pet hospital, if you want to be a veterinarian.

Whatever you decide to do, remember that college and scholarship applications will inquire about summer activities – so, make yours count!

▶ *Counselors*

Counselors are the people in your high school who help you navigate the academic world.

If you are in a well-functioning high school, a schedule for seeing a counselor will be communicated to you. But if your high school is large and the counseling staff is small, you must be proactive to request a meeting yourself, no later than May of each year. The purpose of this meeting is to establish your academic program for the following year.

Remember that your goal is to complete the college prep plan outlined in the beginning of this section.

 Check bulletin boards nearby the Counseling Office for posted information. Many summer programs, college open houses and tours, and scholarship notices are sent to the Counseling Office.

▶ *Know Thyself*

Down the road, you will be expected to write essays for college applications and/or scholarships. For many students, this is a scary prospect; but it need not be a difficult one. You simply need to understand that at the heart of every good college essay is a biographical narrative that tells your story. An easy way to get in touch with your past experiences is to complete a *Biographical Profile* (Appendix C). Once completed,this material can be used to create an insightful narrative about your life's journey. This is what makes for the best college essays!

FRESHMEN: END-OF-YEAR CHECKLIST

Check items accomplished during the year. ✓

Joined a school club and/or participated in athletics program	
Practiced time management, note-taking, study, and test-taking skills	
Completed a *Biographical Profile* (Appendix C)	
Adopted a local college and got on their email list	
Met with your counselor to outline following year's program	
Explore summer activities to participate in (i.e. volunteer work, internship, summer academy, general work)	
Completed an Interest Inventory	
Began program of vocabulary development (freevocabulary.com)	

Rising Sophomore Summer

Check items accomplished during the summer. ✓

Read at least 3 books of your own choosing	
If you travel, keep a journal of your experiences	
Complete an Interest Inventory or Assessment	
Participated in a substantive summer experience.	
Establish a Working Resume to record your activities (Appendix D)	
Explore scholarship websites (see pp. 147–151)	
Take the ACT® Plan Test (if not taken during the year)	

Learn About Higher Education

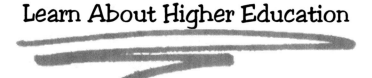

WHAT YOU CAN STUDY

Higher education institutions—two-year and four-year colleges and universities—come in all shapes and sizes. Collectively, there are more than 4,000 such institutions sprinkled throughout the country. They differ one from another by their various programs of study (curricula). Some place emphasis on providing a liberal arts education, while others offer degrees in very specialized areas. Understanding the differences can help you direct your college search in the right direction.

THE LIBERAL ARTS

What is a liberal arts education? Most authorities might agree that a liberal arts education works to develop well-informed and well-rounded individuals by exposing them to a wide range of subject matter. Individuals who undertake a liberal arts education build a capacity to think more broadly and deeply about the world around them and the opportunities and challenges it faces. They become excellent problem-solvers and possess strong speaking, reading and writing skills. This is why a liberal arts education is considered an ideal foundation for those seeking to enter the professions —

medicine, law, teaching, psychology, social work, etc.

At liberal arts institutions, students can "major" or seek a degree in any number of programs. Academic offerings can be quite sweeping, covering everything from Anthropology, Business, Literature, Languages, Mathematics, Psychology, Sociology, to Zoology, just to name a few.

Depending on the size of the institution, liberal arts majors can be organized into schools, departments or divisions. A quick sampling of curricula at three liberal arts institutions produced the following list, and certainly there are more:

Division of Arts and Humanities

Department of the Social Sciences

Division of Behavioral Sciences

Department of Physical Sciences

Department of Natural Sciences

School of Business

School of Education

Department of Health Sciences

Did You Know?

The most prestigious liberal arts colleges and universities throughout the nation are those with Phi Beta Kappa charters.

SCIENCE, TECHNOLOGY, ENGINEERING, MATHEMATICS (STEM)

For students who do well in mathematics and science, it could be said that the world is their oyster. Not only will many future careers demand strong skills in STEM, but growth in employment will also be strongest for those who have this background.

The call for well-prepared students and employees with STEM skill sets has become compelling. "We need STEM-related talent to compete globally, and we will need even more in the future. It is not a matter of choice: For the United States to remain the global innovation leader, we must make the most of all of the potential STEM talent this country has to offer."[4]

Consequently, employees in STEM areas will be able to garner the best salaries and job opportunities as engineers, researchers, statisticians, analysts, scientists, and more. While STEM majors are offered at liberal arts institutions, you may want to attend a research institution that targets study in these disciplines, such as Rensselaer Polytechnic Institute, Georgia Institute of Technology, Massachusetts Institute of Technology (MIT), just to name a few.

THE ARTS

Art, music, theater, design and dance are collectively referred to as "the arts." Students who are especially well trained and wish to pursue a career in the arts may choose to attend a professional school or conservatory, for more rigorous training. Institutions dedicated to arts education, like Juilliard, Parsons School of Design, or the New England Conservatory of Music (just to name a few), are quite selective and require an audition or portfolio as part of the admissions process. So, applying early is a must.

Students who do not have strong training in an artistic discipline, but want to begin or continue studies in the arts while at college, will enjoy attending a liberal arts institution. Here, they can get the best of both worlds –academics and the arts.

Pre-Professional Study

At the undergraduate level, fields of study that generally require graduate school education are often grouped into "pre-professional study" areas. These categories can include, but are not limited to, pre-medical, pre-law, pre-engineering, and pre-social work. Generally, pre-professional advisors are designated to ensure that students prepare for access to graduate or professional schools. Undergraduate advisement can include test prep, interviewing techniques, application guidance, letters of recommendation and more.

VOCATIONAL EDUCATION

Vocational education is an option for many students who wish to study a trade or craft. It encompasses focused *training* that leads to careers as automotive service technicians, cosmetologists, dental assistants, electricians, hair stylists, and plumbers, just to name a few. Many two-year community colleges and for-profit institutions offer vocational training programs.

CREDENTIALS YOU CAN GET

When you have completed a course of study, you will receive a credential that honors your achievement. This may come in the form of a diploma, license or certificate.

Certificates

Completion time	6 months to 2 years
Where offered	Community colleges, vocational or trade schools
Occupations	Cosmetologist, Mechanic, Electrician, Office Skills and more

Associate's Degree (AA, AS, AAS)

Completion time	2 years
Where offered	Community colleges, some vocational or trade schools
Occupations	Dental Hygienists, Programmer, Paralegal and more

Bachelor's Degree (BA, BS, BFA, BE and more)

Completion time	4 years
Where offered	4-year colleges or universities
Occupations	Many jobs require this level of degree for entry to a profession

Master's Degree (MA, MBA, MS, MSW, MFA, M.ED.)

Completion time	2-3 years beyond a Bachelor's degree
Where offered	Colleges with graduate programs
Occupations	Engineers, Teachers, Social Workers, Counselors and more

Doctoral Degree (Ph.D., Ed.D)

Completion time	3-5 years beyond a Master's degree
Where offered	Colleges with doctoral programs
Occupations	Professors, Scientists, Directors, Researchers, Analysts and more

Professional Degree (JD, MD, DDS)

Completion time after college	Law = 3 yrs.; Medicine = 4 yrs. of medical school + 2-5 yrs. Residency; Dentistry = 4 yrs. of dental school + 2 or more yrs. for a specialty
Where offered	Schools of Law, Medicine, Dentistry
Occupations	Lawyers, Medical Doctors, Surgeons, Dentists

TIP — You may want to return to p. 19 to see the *Average Family Income* associated with each degree level, in 2010.

SOPHOMORES

(10th Grade)

Boost Your

Success

Must-know Tips for 10th Grade

It is hoped that you got off to a really great start in your freshman year. If not, hit re-set and begin anew. Remember to set the bar high and work to your personal best.

▶ *Build a Strong GPA*

Hopefully, you are pleased with your performance in freshman year. But, if you feel you can improve, this year is an opportunity to get off to an even better start. Remember, a strong academic record is an important qualifier for college admissions.

Did You Know?

At the end of your junior year, your "college academic average" will be computed exclusively from your "college prep classes." Most colleges will use this average to qualify you for admission.

▶ *The Math Effect*

If you want to get to the best colleges, math can be your ticket. Studies have shown that the more math a student takes in high school, the more prepared he or she is for college-level work. And, strong math preparation allows students to take advantage of a wider range of college majors, such as engineering, architecture, information technology, manufacturing, etc.

Did You Know?

56% of those who took advanced algebra (Algebra II) earned a bachelor's degree vs. 13% who took some algebra and/or geometry.

73% of students who took calculus earned a bachelor's degree compared to 3% who took general or basic math.[5]

▶ *Teacher Connections*

Continue to build strong relationships with your teachers. When you are applying for scholarships and college, you will want to reach back to a few of them for letters of recommendation. A teacher should be able to write more than "Jordan took my class in his sophomore year and scored an 88." Ideally, you want teachers to be able to embellish statements about your personality, relations with fellow students, leadership qualities, and potential for advanced work. Teachers can write powerfully persuasive letters on behalf of students, so let them get to know you. *Make yourself memorable!*

▶ *Practice Tests*

Standardized testing is another important criterion that colleges use in making admission decisions. This year, you can get a feel for the PSAT/NMSQT and the ACT. You want to experience these tests to become familiar with the test instructions and format. This can lower your test jitters when you encounter the real thing, next year.

▶ *Maintain a Personal Budget*

Have you opened a savings account yet? If not, please do so soon and begin depositing monies from gifts, paychecks from work, and scholarship awards.

This year's *new goal* is to maintain a personal budget so that you can monitor your spending and saving habits. Keeping track of money, coming in and going out, improves your awareness of cash flow and helps you set monetary goals. This will position you nicely to handle your own finances when you enter college. A *Personal Budget Worksheet* (Appendix E) is provided in the back of this Guide to help you track your spending and savings activities.

▶ *Continue to Build Your College Fund*

Scholarships are plentiful and all around you. Keep your eyes peeled for notices on bulletin boards in your high school, newspapers, organizations, churches, etc. When you have free time, perform online searches such as "scholarships for high school students," "scholarships for minority students," "scholarships for students with disabilities," etc.

Be creative in designing your own scholarship search strings. Remember an application and essay are usually required.

▶ *Develop a Resume*

It is a good idea to begin a working resume that lists your work and volunteer experiences, summer activities, and accomplishments. When listing information, you are required to include places where activities took place, as well as dates of participation. Once you create your resume, you should update it at least once a year. For your convenience, a *Resume Template* (Appendix D) is available in the back of this Guide.

▶ *Use Social Media Wisely*

Think they won't look? Think again! College admissions staff are increasingly scanning social media sites to screen prospective student activities. Their concerns run the gamut from posted hate speech, cheating, and references to substance abuse, just to name a few. You want to remember that colleges are interested to admit students who exercise good judgment and won't expose their institution to unwarranted scandals. This stealth review, on the part of colleges, won't be apparent to you so begin now to be thoughtful about your posts, tweets and pics. In other words, keep it clean!

▶ *Counselor Connection*

If a meeting with a counselor has not been scheduled, please request one *no later* than May of this year. The purpose of this session is to discuss and plan next year's academic programming. Remember that your goal is to complete a college prep program as outlined on pp. 38-39.

▶ *Summer Exploration*

Consider using this summer to take advantage of a workshop, internship or other enrichment program. As they tap into your interests, these programs often incorporate career exploration and social activities. You'll find summer program offerings usually at educational institutions, so look around in your surrounding area.

You can also locate programs online by searching "summer programs for high school students," "summer programs in mathematics for high school students," "summer programs in theater for high school students," just to name a few. Use your interests and create your own search strings.

If work is your desired choice for the summer, it is a good idea to look for an environment where you can learn *new skills* that will be beneficial to your continued development.

Sophomores: End-of-Year Checklist

Check items accomplished during the year. ✓

	✓
Joined a school club and/or participated in athletics program	
Practiced good time management, note-taking, study, and test-taking skills	
Took **ACT° Plan** test	
Maintained a *Personal Budget Worksheet* (Appendix E)	
Took a **practice PSAT** test (cannot be used for National Merit Scholarship Program)	
Attended college admissions forums	
Took **SAT Subject Tests**	
Met with a counselor to plan junior year program, including honors classes, if appropriate	
Select a substantive summer experience to participate in (i.e. volunteer work, internship, summer academy, general work)	
Developed a *Resume* (Appendix D)	

Rising Junior Summer

Check items accomplished during the summer. ✓

	✓
Read at least 3 books of your own choosing	
If you travel, keep a journal to capture your experiences	
Participate in a substantive summer experience	
Re-take Interest Inventory Assessment	
Complete a Career Assessment	
Visit local colleges	
Update Resume (Appendix D)	

What You Need to Know about College Admissions

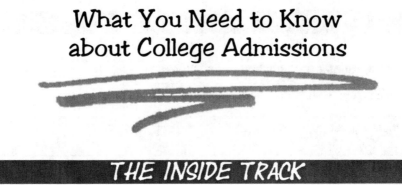

THE INSIDE TRACK

The topics covered in this section are given special attention because they are so important to the discussion of college preparation and admissions. You will want to review these topics thoroughly, *before* you enter the college search phase.

▶ *PSAT PATHWAY TO NATIONAL MERIT®* *SCHOLARSHIP PROGRAM*

The most celebrated role of the PSAT is to serve as a preparatory test for the SAT. But the PSAT has another function as well – it can qualify students for the **National Merit Scholarship Program.** If you have been doing very well in high school and are expected to perform well on the PSAT, you will want to consult with your counselor about the possibility of entering the competition for scholarships, *by your junior year*.

For more information: Visit http://www.nationalmerit. org/nmsp.php#entryreq.

▶ *COLLEGE ON LITTLE-TO-NO DEBT*

TWO-TO-FOUR-YEAR COLLEGE PIPELINE

Many students are reducing the overall cost of attending college by choosing *first* to attend a two-year institution or community college. The tuition at two-year colleges, especially those in the public sector, is cheaper than that at four-year colleges. And, if you do very well, you can qualify for scholarships upon graduation with an associate's degree. These scholarships will, in turn, lower the cost of attendance when you transfer to a four-year institution.

If this strategy seems attractive, investigate the four-year college you wish to attend *before* you seek entry. This will insure that you know ahead of time that the four-year institution will accept most, if not all, of your transfer credits.

Another way to safeguard your credits in the transfer transaction is to pursue an associate's degree in the liberal arts. These credits transfer most easily between institutions and create a great foundation for upper-division courses taken at a four-year college. Above all, it is very important that you do not lose credits in the transfer process, which could be costly and defeat the overall purpose of this strategy.

PUBLIC-TO-PRIVATE PIPELINE

There is no doubt that public colleges and universities have markedly reduced tuition rates compared to those in the private sector. If family circumstances do not permit you to pay for college as you go, without the use of loans, then attending a public institution (city or state) with a great reputation is the best alternative. You need not sacrifice quality by taking this step — some of the best colleges and universities are to be found in the public sector.

Choosing to attend a public institution is an excellent strategy for those who expect to pursue graduate or professional education – such as aspiring doctors, lawyers, teachers, engineers, psychologists, etc. *You will lower educational costs at the undergraduate level, so that the debt-clock will not start ticking (if at all) until much later in your educational experience.* You can always elect to attend a private institution or Ivy at the graduate level, if this is what you have your heart set on.

Low-income Students CAN Attend Ivies?

High-achieving students from low-income households do not need to give up on their dream of attending an Ivy League college. To the contrary, these institutions are especially interested in strengthening their student diversity by including gifted students from the lower end of the income spectrum. Whether it is Brown, Columbia, Cornell, Dartmouth, Harvard, U Penn, Princeton or Yale, each college has designed financial aid packaging to make it feasible for low-income students to attend. So, if you have a strong academic record, you should definitely include at least one Ivy in your college application mix.

ROTC Programs

Offered at more than 1,000 colleges and universities across the United States, the Reserve Officers' Training Corps (ROTC) prepares young adults to become U.S. military officers. In exchange for a paid college education and a guaranteed post-college career, cadets commit to serve in the military after graduation.

Generally, the service obligation for the Army is eight years; the Navy, five years; the Marine Corps, four years; and the Air Force, four to ten years.

ROTC students attend college like other students, but also receive basic military training and officer training for their chosen branch of service through the ROTC unit at or nearby the college.[6]

▶ THE BEST COLLEGE IS???

In short, the best college is the right college for YOU! It is the college that embraces your academic and social interests, while also meeting your financial needs. This formula may mean that you will find the right college in the public sector, at city- or state-funded institutions with lower tuition rates. Or, you might find an institution within the pricier private sector. What is most important is to pinpoint the institution that suits you best. You will know it because it will feel "right" and have most, if not all, of what you are looking for. In the end, this will be your best college!

▶ *STUDENT-ATHLETES*

There are specific designations for institutions that offer athletic programs for student-athletes. The National Collegiate Athletic Association (NCAA) is a nonprofit organization that sets rules for participating colleges and universities. Some 1200 institutions across the nation are assigned to divisions based on the aggregate number of sports, number of athletes and the number of teams that play against each other in the same division. The number of schools that participate in each division[7] are listed as follows:

Division I   –   340 institutions

Division II   –   290 institutions

Division III   –   436 institutions

▶ *FACTORS IN ADMISSION DECISIONS*

Every year, the National Association for College Admissions Counseling (NACAC) surveys college admissions offices about their previous year's admission practices. The results are collated and organized into a report that includes the ranking of top factors in college admission decisions.

Here are the results from the *State of College Admission Report*[8] for 2013:

1. Grades in college prep courses
2. Strength of curriculum
3. Admission test scores (SAT, ACT)
4. Grades in all courses
5. Essay or writing sample
6. Student's demonstrated interest
7. Counselor recommendation
8. Teacher recommendation
9. Class Rank
10. Extracurricular activities
11. Interview
12. Portfolio
13. Subject test scores (AP, IB)
14. SAT II scores
15. State graduation exam scores
16. Work

▶ *SCHOLARSHIPS · HONORS COLLEGES · HONORS PROGRAMS*

Scholarships are available through a variety of sources – unions, civic associations, corporate organizations, state and local governments, fraternities and sororities, and more. In addition to these sources, remember that colleges offer scholarships to incoming freshmen, too. Generally, these will be merit-based awards that take into account student grades and test scores. Scholarships of this type can range from partial to full-tuition awards that can be used only at the issuing college. And, if you are granted an award and it is renewable, you will be expected to maintain a minimum grade point average (GPA) in order to keep it from one year to the next. A *Scholarship Tracking Form* is available in the back of this Guide to help you keep track of all scholarships that you apply to (Appendix I).

When you visit campuses, be sure to ask about scholarship eligibility criteria and application procedures. This information is also carried on college Admissions and Financial Aid web pages.

Honors Colleges have sprung up at many colleges and universities in the past fifteen to twenty years. Designed to reward academic excellence, they have a mission to provide the best model for advanced teaching and learning for top-notch students. They usually offer full tuition and a variety of perks, such as accelerated classes, small class sizes, stipends for books and study abroad opportunities. It is important to know that there is usually a separate application process for honors college admission, so be sure to ask about the process and plan to apply early. *If you are working hard and achieving super results, this can be your ticket to getting a debt-free college education!*

Honors Programs are offered at most, if not all, institutions and provide an accelerated learning experience for strong students who enjoy working at an advanced level. Students usually apply for the program *after* they have been admitted to the institution; candidates need to present strong high school averages, letters of recommendations and meet other criteria. But honors programs *do not* grant monetary awards.

▶ *"EARLY ACTION" or "EARLY DECISION"*

Admission programs known as "early action" and "early decision" are attractive for two primary reasons. First, they allow students to apply early and get early admission notifications. Students can apply as early as November and get a decision notice as early as December. In contrast, students applying in the regular admission pool usually apply by March and get admission notification on or about April 1st. Second, students applying early can have up to a *20% edge in gaining acceptance* to an institution, over those who apply during the regular admission phase with *exactly the same* academic profile.

Before you decide to pursue one of these options, please weigh the advantages associated with each program:

Early Action permits a student to apply early and get an early acceptance, usually by January. However, the student does not have to make a commitment to attend the school until around May 1st, which is the normal notification date for all colleges. Students using this option can take advantage of higher admission rates without jeopardizing their other college choices.

Early Decision is much like the "early action" option in that a student applies early and gets an early admission decision. But, if admitted, the student <u>must accept</u> the admission invitation. Parents and students sign a binding agreement to this effect. The drawback here is that a student must drop all other college offers and therefore cannot compare financial aid packages. Given the exclusive nature of this option, it is appropriate *only* for a student who has identified a "dream" school and, if admitted, is absolutely willing to attend.

Quick Reference Chart

Admission Program	Application Deadline	Admission Decision	Advantages	Drawbacks
Early Action	Nov. or Dec.	Dec. or Jan.	Higher admission rates Do not have to accept until May 1st	none
Early Decision	Nov. or Dec.	Dec. or Jan.	Higher admission rates	Must accept admission invitation Cannot review other financial aid packages
Regular Admission	March	April 1st (approx.)	Do not have to accept until May 1st	Lower admission rate than Early Action/Early Decision

▶ *PROPRIETARY EDUCATION*

Institutions in the "for-profit" education sector are known as "proprietary institutions." They generally offer vocational and career-driven programs that are short-term and certificate-based. Traditional-aged freshmen may not find this education model attractive, because few student-oriented amenities are available, such as student activities, sports programs, student government, etc. For this reason, these institutions tend to appeal more to adult learners.

Additionally, proprietary institutions are known to have high tuition rates, requiring many applicants to sign up for hefty loans. For this reason, do your homework carefully. First, you might want to see if the program you are seeking is offered at a public community college. Before signing on, you should ask a few questions: How are students prepared for jobs? A year out from graduation, what are the employment rates for alumni? Which employers recruit the institution's graduates?

While many institutions operate in a principled way, some use deceptive recruiting practices to lure students into risky loan arrangements. A hard sell and/or suggestion that you should lie on a financial aid application should be a clue to run in the opposite direction.

▶ *FACULTY & RESEARCH*

Beware the marketing of "star" faculty. Some institutions attempt to lure you to their campuses with pronouncements about their high-profile professors without telling you that it is unlikely that you can take class with them, because they teach only at the graduate level.

You want to know what opportunities exist for you to engage in research activities, either student-led with faculty guidance or assisting faculty in their projects. It is also important to ask how early you can engage in research. In the event that research opportunities are not available early on, you should seek out math and science clubs, honors programs, opportunities to attend academic conferences and/or participate in undergraduate academic contests like the William Lowell Putnam Mathematical Competition.

▶ *COLLEGE RANKINGS*

Every year, commercial publications, most notably *U.S. News & World Report, Forbes,* and Princeton Review, issue college ratings. These highly publicized rankings draw lots of public attention, especially during the college search season, and generally assess institutions based on how much money their fund-raising efforts can boast of and how much they spend on their physical plant and faculty salaries. But these factors do not provide prospective students with the information they really need to know to make an informed decision. A school's graduation rate, job placement rate, and student admissions to professional and graduate schools tell you much more about your prospects if you attend that very institution.

This is not to say that there is no value in screening college rankings promoted by the major publications. But other college assessments should be added to the mix. Fortunately, a number of guides with more realistic assessments are available. Simply make a trip to your school or public library and browse the stacks devoted to college preparation and admissions. You are sure to become acquainted with a wealth of informative resources there.

And *before* running with the recommendations of any one guide that lists "top ten this" or "top ten that," consult research guides that focus on providing detailed information about colleges without a rating system. Publications in this category include *Peterson's Guide to Colleges*, *Barron's Profiles of American Colleges*, *Fiske Guide to Colleges*, and others that you can also find in your local library.

At the end of the day, your top 10 college list should reflect the homework that you executed among many resources, not just the most popular ones.

▶ *COLLEGE SELECTIVITY*

Reference is often made to a *college's selectivity*. Essentially, this refers to how competitive you can expect a college's admission requirements to be. Here's how it works. If a college admits few freshmen out of a large applicant pool, the freshmen selected will have the strongest academic profiles (grades and test scores). The higher the grades and testing scores of admitted freshmen, the higher the selectivity rating is likely to be for the institution. Institutions are usually termed most selective, very selective, highly selective, selective, least selective or open admissions.

STANDARDIZED TESTING

SAT I® & ACT®

Most colleges will accept both the **SAT I** and the **ACT**, so it is wise to take both exams. Many students find that they score better on one exam than the other. The possible reason for this lies in the differences in the tests make-up. The ACT assesses what a student actually learned in the classroom, while the SAT assesses reasoning and verbal abilities.

A college is especially interested to see these standardized test scores because they want to identify students who have a strong potential to do well in college. On the following page are the differences between the tests.

SAT vs. ACT

Test format	Critical Reading, Math, Writing	English, Math, Reading, Science, Writing (optional)
Math	Basic Arithmetic Algebra I Algebra II Geometry	Pre-Algebra Algebra I Algebra II Geometry Trigonometry
Science	None	Data Representation Research and Science Reading Charts Experiments
Reading	Sentence Completions Reading comprehension based on long and short excerpts	Four passages: Prose Fiction, Social Science, Humanities, Natural Science
Writing	One Essay Grammar Usage Word Choice	Usage and Mechanics Grammar Sentence Improvement Optional Writing: Essay
Length	3 hr. 45 min.	2 hr 55 min + 30 min for writing
Penalty for Wrong Answer	Yes	No
Fee (2014)	Yes - $51 includes writing section	Yes - $38 plus $16 for writing (optional)
Fee waivers	Check with high school counselor	Check with high school counselor
Request scores	www.collegeboard.org	www.actstudent.org

SAT II Subject Tests™

Many private colleges and honors colleges require a set number of **SAT II Subject Tests.** It is recommended that you take 2-3 SAT II's in subjects where you do especially well.

The best rule of thumb is to take an SAT II test in the spring term of the year you take the course. This will ensure your best performance as the class material will be fresh to you.

At this writing, SAT II Subject Tests are offered by the College Board in the following areas:

Literature

U.S. History

World History

Math Level 1 (take after 2 years of algebra and 1 year of geometry)

Math Level 2 (take after 2 years of algebra, 1 year of geometry and precalculus and/or trigonometry)

Biology/EM

Chemistry

Physics

French

French with Listening

German

German with Listening

Spanish

Spanish with Listening

Modern Hebrew

Italian

Latin

Chinese with Listening

Japanese with Listening

Korean with Listening

Fee (2014): **$51 per test**

For more information: Download the "Getting Ready for the SAT Subject Tests" booklet at http://sat.collegeboard.org/about-tests/sat-subject-tests.

Advanced Placement Program (AP®)

For the *best* prepared students, the **Advanced Placement Program** (AP) is an attractive option for senior year programming. At last count, the College Board listed 34 AP offerings. With a strong score on an AP exam, students can reap college credit or advanced placement in college courses. This is not an option for everyone, but juniors with very strong academic records should discuss this option with a counselor.

For more information: Download the "Put AP to Work for You" at https://apstudent.collegeboard.org/exploreap/the-rewards.

To sit for SAT I, ACT and a few SAT Subject Tests can range **from $138.50 to $256.50**. Be sure to grow your college fund to cover these fees.

FACTORS TO CONSIDER WHEN CHOOSING A COLLEGE

1. ACADEMIC REPUTATION – Colleges or universities are usually best known for a handful of premier programs. While an institution may offer 50 or so majors, it is really known to be superior in possibly 12. Your goal is to match your academic interests to an institution that offers the best education in that field.

2. ACADEMIC ADVISEMENT – One of the most important college resources that should be available to you, from day one, is academic advisement. This service is provided by academic advisors who help you plan your academic program, from one semester to the next. They also provide referrals to other programs and services, as needed. Ultimately, they will ensure that you are completing all the requirements of your degree program, so that you can graduate on time.

3. GRADUATION RATE – The graduation rate tells how many students graduate in four or six years from an institution. This rate is an indicator of the institutional support provided to students to ensure that they fulfill their degree requirements in a timely fashion.

4. COST – The cost of college is a serious consideration, *but* it should not be the *only* factor in determining where you will enroll. All colleges have financial aid programs to help you meet the cost of attending. The one caution here is that if you will be required to take out loans to finance the bulk of your education, you should probably consider a more affordable college option.

5. CAMPUS LIFE – When you go to college, a relatively small portion of your time is actually spent in classes. Most of your time will be spent in the library, laboratories, dorms, student centers, cafeterias, and other places where students congregate. On your visits to the campus, try to get a feel for how and where students mingle.

6. COED OR SINGLE-SEX – The overwhelming majority of colleges are coed, attended by both males and females. However, many single-sex colleges are popular, preferred by some students for the special attention they receive and the schools' higher graduation rates.

7. LOCATION – Do you want to live on campus or at home? Do you want to go away to school, perhaps to another state? Do you prefer to live in a rural, suburban, or urban environment? Do you prefer a cold climate? These are just some of the questions that you need to answer for yourself when selecting a college location.

8. DIVERSITY – Many institutions are very diverse (racially, ethnically, religiously, on the basis of gender orientation, etc.) while others are predominantly of one group or another. Whichever environment you choose, it is important to know that the institution embraces and respects *all* who attend, and requires the same of its students, administrative staff, buildings and grounds keepers and faculty. To be sure, ask questions of campus officials and speak directly with students and alumni. Campus newspapers can also provide a window into the campus climate.

9. SAFETY – As a result of the "Campus Security Act" (1990), all institutions of higher education are required to collect and make public statistics concerning *crime on campus* and steps taken to prevent crime. Visit the U.S. Department of Education's website on Campus Safety at www.ope.ed.gov/security to get up-to-date crime statistics on *any* college campus.

10. SIZE – There are different advantages to small, medium and large colleges. Small colleges offer a more personalized experience, while large ones offer a greater variety of academic options, athletics and social events. The important thing is to decide what feels most comfortable to YOU.

JUNIORS

(11ᵗʰ Grade)

College Search

Begins

Must-know Tips for 11th Grade

This is the year that you are expected to begin college search activities in earnest. The material in this section will acquaint you with the fundamentals and provide a timetable and action plan for implementation.

▶ *PSAT Testing*

Upon returning to school, immediately contact your counselor to sign up to take the **October PSAT.**

High scores on this exam may qualify you for consideration in the *National Merit Scholarship Program* and/or the *National Achievement Scholarship Program* for Black Students. The *National Hispanic Recognition Program* uses this October test to acknowledge outstanding Hispanic/Latino students.

Did You Know?

In your junior year, you should take a *minimum* of two standardized tests:

1) the **PSAT** in the fall term, and

2) the **SAT I** in the spring term.

▶ *College Exploration*

1. College brochures and email messages will begin to flood in soon after you take the PSAT. When you have time, begin to explore this material to familiarize yourself with college offerings. Look for a *Freshman Profile* that identifies the academic qualifications for students who gained admission to an institution in the recent past.

If a Profile is not readily available, check the website or ask the school to provide one.

2. Begin thinking about what will matter most to you in selecting a college. Revisit the *Top 10 Factors to Consider When Choosing A College* on pp. 77-79, to qualify your preferences.

3. A list of "Useful College Websites" (Appendix B) should be an additional tool for your review when exploring colleges and specific aspects of college search.

4. Develop a list of 7 to 10 institutions to investigate when you are given the opportunity to attend college fairs or make college visits. If you performed the research suggested in Step 1 and identified your preferences in Step 2, then you are ready to get the most out of college visits and meetings with college representatives.

▶ *Teacher, Counselor & Family Connections*

Your junior year is the best time to begin reaching out to your teachers, counselors and college-educated family members for their insights and opinions about colleges, in general.

You might ask them to share information about their own college experiences and what they believe is important to weigh in today's college decision-making.

▶ *Career Exploration*

The more you know about the career you want to undertake, the more focused your college search can be. For example, if you are serious about becoming an engineer, you will want to search for colleges with strong engineering programs. If becoming a teacher is your goal, then a college with a solid liberal arts education and teacher preparation program is what you should seek.

However, if you don't yet know what you want to do with the rest of your life, *don't panic.*

Take advantage of the opportunity to explore careers through the *Occupational Outlook Handbook* (Bureau of Labor) at http://bls.gov/ooh.

▶ *College Fairs & Visitations*

You will want to attend as many local college fairs, campus tours, and open houses as you can reasonably schedule over the course of the fall and spring terms. At these events, you will have the opportunity to speak directly with college representatives.

Be sure to also schedule visits to college campuses. Remember, it is important to establish a "fit" with a college – the place where you will spend the majority of your time over the next two to four years. So, you must experience the environment firsthand to determine if it is right for you.

"Scheduling College Visits" (Appendix F) is a form that helps you schedule and organize your college visits. A "College Data Chart" (Appendix H) helps you log information received for easy comparison of institutions. Suggested "Campus Visit Questions" (Appendix G) should be reviewed in advance and taken along on any college visit.

▶ *Time to Write*

It's time to prepare for the activity of writing essays. These writing samples may be required as part of the freshman application and/or scholarship process. While you do not yet know the topics that you will be asked to address, in most cases you can anchor your text to a solidly written biographical narrative that tells who you are, what your notable accomplishments and challenges have been, and what your short- and long-term goals are. If you haven't already done so, complete the *Biographical Profile* (Appendix C). This will help to unlock your memories and serve as a foundation for your biographical narrative.

▶ *SAT I and ACT Testing*

Your first opportunity to take the SAT I and the ACT will occur in the spring of your junior year. You won't want to miss this opportunity to see how you perform, before you retake these tests in the fall term of your senior year.

Also, in the spring term, you should take 1-2 **SAT II Subject Tests.** For more information, see the section on "Standardized Testing" on pp. 74-75.

▶ *Counselor Connection*

Your counselor meeting, in the spring of this year, is vital to establishing your senior year program. The first concern to address is to see that you have completed all required courses to put you on track for graduation. If not, adjustments should be made to ensure this result.

Second, if you have done exceptionally well in some classes (usually at the honors level), you should seek to take *Advanced Placement (AP®)* classes. Strong performance in these classes is valued in the college selection process, especially for scholarship consideration.

And strong scores on AP exam(s) may earn college credit and/or advanced standing in college courses from an institution.

▶ *Letters of Recommendations*

Begin giving thought to whom you want to approach for letters of recommendation. You may want to alert these teachers and counselors that you plan to reach out to them in the fall of your senior year.

▶ *Summer Challenge*

This is your *last opportunity* to take advantage of a summer enrichment program that will permit you to investigate your primary field of interest. Remember, this experience can help you refine your choice of a college major. The better matched you are to a major, the more likely you are to select a college that is right for you.

JUNIOR YEAR CALENDAR

FALL	To-Do List	✓
September	Contact counseling office to sign-up for PSAT/NMSQT*	
October	Take **PSAT/NMSQT***	
	Attend college fairs, campus tours, open houses (including HS college night)	
November	Familiarize yourself with financial aid terminology (pp. 108-113)	
	Attend college fairs, campus tours, open houses (including HS college night)	
December	Develop a *Biographical Narrative*	
	Explore the *Occupational Outlook Handbook* at http://bls.gov/ooh	
Fall term	Scholarship search (pp. 65-66, 149-150)	

SPRING	To-Do List	✓
January	Sign-up for *My College QuickStart* for SAT study plan and college exploration (http://www.collegeboard.com/student/testing/psat/about.html)	
February	Attend a financial aid workshop	
March	Attend a financial aid workshop	
	Register to take the SAT I in May.	
April	Register to take the SAT I in June (if not in March)	
	Take **SAT II Subject Tests**	
	Meet with counselor to discuss senior year classes and, if appropriate, include AP and Honors classes in the senior year program.	
	Plan Summer activities (i.e. internships, academic summer programs/workshops, community service, work).	
May or June	Take **SAT I** and/or **ACT Test**	
Spring term	Scholarship search (see above)	

JUNIORS: END-OF-YEAR CHECKLIST

Check items accomplished during the year	✓
Joined a school club and/or participated in athletics program	
Took the **PSAT/NMSQT** in October	
Attended college fairs, tours, open houses	
Signed up for *My College QuickStart*	
Took **SAT I** in the spring term	
Took **ACT** in the spring term	
Maintained a Personal Budget (Appendix E)	
Met with Counselor to outline senior year program, adding challenging courses as appropriate	
Updated Diploma Requirements Worksheet	
Took SAT Subject Tests	
Attended a financial aid workshop	
Developed a *Biographical Narrative*	
Searched scholarships online and with parents.	
Explored the *Occupational Outlook Handbook*	

RISING SENIOR SUMMER

Check items accomplished during the summer	✓
Participate in a summer internship, workshop or academic program	
Read at least 3 books of your own choosing	
Visit as many colleges as possible	
If you travel, keep a journal of your experiences	
Participate in a substantive summer experience.	
Update Resume (Appendix D)	
Register to take the **ACT** and **SAT I** tests in October or November	
Establish a Filing System to organize college materials	

Get Ready For Senior Year

ORGANIZE, ORGANIZE, ORGANIZE

The most important step you can take to minimize senior year frenzy is to get yourself well organized. Remember, you will need to manage assorted applications, personal documentation, deadlines, attendance at events, and much more – all while continuing to hold down your senior year studies. Here are some suggested procedures to put in place <u>before</u> senior year begins.

I. Sort College Materials

Obtain 3 boxes able to hold 11" wide documents.

Label each box as "most", "some" and "little".

Sort college catalogs and brochures as follows:

Box 1 – colleges of *most* interest

Box 2 – colleges of *some* interest

Box 3 – colleges of *little* interest

You may find that material will move from one box to another, as you learn more about institutions. So, don't be too quick to throw away materials.

II. Establish a Filing System

Purchase and label 10 folders as follows:

FOLDER NAME	WHAT TO INSERT
Writing Samples	Copies of essays, resume, biographical narrative
References	Letters of recommendation, Student Activity Form
Academic Documents	Copies of high school transcript, original test scores (PSAT, SAT I, ACT and SAT II Subject Tests)
Scholarship Outreach	Scholarship Tracking Form
College Visitations	Campus Visitation Tracking Form, College Visit Form
Financial Aid	Copy of FAFSA, SAR and supporting documents
College Notifications	All college acceptance and rejection letters
College Selection	College Selection Form
Freshman Transition	Freshman Transition Form
Miscellaneous	Other

Note: All forms are provided in the Appendices section of this Guide.

III. On-the-Go

Purchase an expanding folder with multiple pockets to serve as your *On-the-Go* carry item. This will be useful to you when you transport materials to campus offices or retrieve materials.

SENIORS

(12th Grade)

Manage College

Admission Process

Must-know Tips for 12th Grade

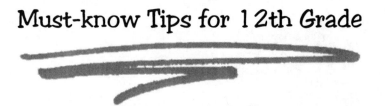

You've made it to your last year! As exciting as this prospect is, this is the year when you must accomplish a number of tasks to successfully gain a freshman seat in the college of your choice. You will want to review this section repeatedly to ensure that you don't miss any key information. And you will want to utilize the tools supplied in the Appendix section for your convenience. The game is on – stay focused and go all out!

▶ *Do Your Homework*

Check out many independent resources to learn about colleges you are seriously considering. Your school library and public libraries in your neighborhood will carry any number of publications to help you become informed about colleges at-large, the college admission process, scholarships, and financial aid.

▶ *College Choices*

Your goal is to narrow your choices to **6 to 9 colleges** to apply to. If you've done your homework well, this will not be difficult. *Why so few colleges?* Keep in mind that each freshman application requires a fee, which can range from **$50 to $75 per application**.

It is recommended that 6 to 9 colleges be distributed as follows:

Safe Schools	Where you are sure to be admitted	2-3 choices
Desired Schools	Where you would accept admission, if not accepted to one of your dream schools	3-4 choices
Dream School	The *most competitive* colleges you apply to and, if accepted, you would *definitely* attend	1-2 choices

▶ *Visitations to Colleges*

The fall term is your *last chance* to see colleges. Make every effort to visit colleges so that you are not picking one sight unseen. Nothing beats being able to walk the grounds, visit the cafeteria and dorms and speak with students. If you can't travel to an out-of-town campus, see if a video tour is available on the college website. Forms are available to facilitate scheduling visits and recording your impressions – see Appendixes F, G, H.

▶ *Standardized Testing*

Take the **SAT I** and the **ACT** exams *no later* than November. This will allow you to submit updated scores to colleges and scholarship programs with early deadlines.

If you have not taken any **SAT II Subject Tests,** you want to schedule those in the fall term. If you qualify for **Advanced Placement Program (AP®)** classes, testing will take place at the end of the year.

See "Standardized Testing" section on pp. 72-76 of this Guide, to get detailed information on all testing programs.

▶ *College Applications*

Most colleges want you to complete freshman applications online. Immediately, note the **Deadline Date** for submission of the application and other materials. Then, get your application fee payments in order, and make a list of the documents that you or your high school must submit to the college. This list will likely include an academic transcript, standardized test results, college essay, letters of recommendation, and more.

Don't forget that many **Honors Colleges** have a separate application. Be sure to contact the college or program for admission materials and instructions.

▶ *Beware Senioritis*

Your senior year will be very demanding but this cannot be an excuse for slacking in your academic studies. It is common knowledge now that many colleges will ask for mid-year and end-year senior transcripts. And every year, there are the heartbreaking stories of students who had their college acceptance rescinded due to underwhelming academic performance in the senior year. *Don't let this happen to you!*

▶ *The Undecided Major*

Not sure what major to pursue in college? No problem! The ideal place to start your college education would be at a liberal arts institution, which will expose you to a broad range of academic offerings – one of which is sure to grab your attention. You can indicate "undecided" when asked to name a "major."

It is also important to know that if you attend a four-year college, you do not need to select a major until around your junior year. With the exception of pre-medical and possibly pre-engineering and pre-architectural studies, this lets you use the first two years to complete requirements and sample coursework freely, before you are expected to commit to a major.

▶ *College Essays & Writing Samples*

The general rule of thumb concerning writing a college essay is to paint a picture of yourself, above and beyond the black-and-white data of your academic records. It is *your* personal take on your strengths and weaknesses, ability to overcome challenges that you may have encountered, and expression of your hopes and dreams, that gives life to a good essay. At the same time, you must be sure to address the topic that is presented to you. It is also an excellent idea to get your hands on a college essay writing guide or two to assist you with this assignment.

You do not want to write your essay at the last minute because it *must* be well written. So, be sure to have someone with solid English skills read and edit it before you submit it. Keep in mind that if an interview is not required, your essay will be the main event that represents you.

▶ *Letters of Recommendations*

The moment you have college applications in hand, check to see how many letters of recommendation are requested. Then, reach out to your preferred list of teachers and counselors for these documents. *Be sure to give your references enough time to write a thoughtful letter on your behalf.*

▶ *Scholarships*

Continue to build your college fund. Many more scholarships are available to high school seniors. Don't forget to have your parent(s) check their workplaces for scholarships, as some unions offer awards to members' children.

▶ *Organize, Organize, Organize*

The better organized you are by September of this year, the less likely it is that you will feel overwhelmed by the college admissions process that will unfold over the course of the year.

SENIOR YEAR CALENDAR

FALL	To-Do List	✓
September	**Register for the SAT I and Subject Tests at <u>www.sat.collegeboard.com</u> or the ACT at <u>www.actstudent.org</u>.**	
	Sign-on to scholarship, college information and financial aid websites for regularized updates	
	Request freshman, scholarship and honors colleges' applications.	
	Start completing college applications online	
	Update Resume	
	Attend college Open Houses and Information Sessions	
October	Take the SAT I, and/or ACT	
	Take SAT II Subject Tests	
	Request *at least* 1 counselor and 3 teacher recommendations. Provide your *Student Activity Form* (Appendix J). *Don't wait until the last minute to ask!*	
	Attend college Open Houses and Information Sessions	
	Prepare Early Decision and/or Early Action applications (if desired)	
	Begin writing and polishing essays	
	Pay close attention to high school College Office deadlines.	
	Attend a financial aid workshop	
November	Take the SAT I and/or ACT, *only if not taken in October.*	
	Submit Early Decision and/or Early Action applications (if applicable)	
	Ask someone to review your essays and continue to polish	
	Attend college Open Houses and Information Sessions	
	Before the Thanksgiving break, check on the status of your teacher and counselor recommendations	
December	Submit all college applications to HS Counselor by stated deadlines or directly to colleges as posted deadlines indicate.	

SPRING	To-Do List	✓
January,	Submit FAFSA online at www.fafsa.ed.gov after January 1st.	
February/ March	Check with Counselor to be sure mid-year grades are sent to colleges	
	Prepare and file family household taxes	
	Make sure filing system is in place to organize college responses, financial aid process & scholarship materials.	
April	Attend campus receptions at the colleges where you were admitted for one final look. Use *College Data Chart* (Appendix K) to track acceptances.	
May	*May 1st* is National College Notification Day so be prepared to notify all colleges of your admission decision and mail the deposit to the college of your choice.	
March, April May and June	Pay close attention to deadlines set by the college for submission of important documents, i.e. final transcript, immunization record, room deposits, etc. And attend all freshman advisement and registration activities, as instructed. Use *Freshman Transition Form* to track your progress (Appendix L).	

Time To Write!

SAMPLES OF WRITING REQUIREMENTS

For many students, the most dreaded part of the application process is "writing the essay" (or personal statement, writing sample or descriptive statement). Yes, this part of the application comes in many forms and it is important for you to interpret the requirement properly.

To help you with this assignment, samples of each type of writing requirement have been provided here. These have been extracted from a variety of actual college applications, including some from very prestigious institutions.

It is recommended that you try your hand at drafting a few of them, in advance of the *real thing*. With practice, you will be surprised that the task of getting 500 words on paper really is not that difficult when the subject is YOU. And, if you previously completed the biographical narrative, you have a running start. Remember: <u>Before</u> you release the essay, you must have someone proofread it so that it is well polished.

Essays

A. Please provide a brief essay (200-350 words) choosing one of the following topics:

1. My generation is more (or less) responsible than my parent's generation.
2. The world is a better (or worse) place because of the computer chip.
3. A discussion of your educational and career goals or significant personal experiences.
4. The arts are a necessity, like food and water, for true civilization.

B. Choose one of the following essay topics and enclose a short (500 words or less) typed personal essay:

a. Identify a social or political issue that concerns you and explain what action you have taken in your community.
b. For more than 100 years, Bennett has been educating women, many of whom have become role models in family life and business. What woman, not in your family, do you most admire, and why?
c. Discuss some issue of personal, local, national, or international concern and its importance to you.
d. Evaluate a significant experience, achievement, risk you have taken, or ethical dilemma you have faced and its impact on you.

C. Please write a personal essay telling the Admissions Committee more about yourself. The essay will personalize your application and provide the committee with insight beyond your academic credentials (250 to 500 words).

D. Please write a brief essay about the person, place, or event that has had the greatest influenceon your life.

E. Provide your response to Essay A or B. Please keep a 500-word limit.

Essay A – Life brings many disappointments as well as satisfactions. Could you tell us about a time in your life when you experienced disappointment, or faced difficult or trying circumstances? How did you react?

Essay B – An application to College X is much more than a set of test scores, grades, and activities. It's often a reflection of an applicant's dreams and aspirations, dreams shaped by the worlds we inhabit. We'd like to know a bit more about your world. Describe the world you come from, for example your family, clubs, school, community, city, or town. How has that world shaped your dreams and aspirations?

PERSONAL STATEMENTS

A. This section of the application helps us become acquainted with you in ways different from courses, grades, test scores, and other objective data. It will demonstrate your ability to organize thoughts and express yourself. We are looking for an essay that will help us know you better as a person and as a student. Please write an essay (250-500 words) on a topic of your choice or one of the following options listed.

1. Evaluate a significant experience, achievement, risk you have taken or ethical dilemma you have faced and its impact on you.

2. Discuss some issue of personal, local, national or international concern and its importance to you.

3. Indicate a person who has had a significant influence on you, and describe that influence.

B. Discuss how well your academic record reflects your ability and motivation. 2) Describe a significant experience or achievement that has meaning to you. 3) Discuss your goals for the future and how Cazenovia College can assist you in reaching them. Describe a character in fiction, an historical figure, or a creative work (as in art, music, science, etc.) that has had an influence on you, and explain that influence.

C. *Personal Statement/Essay*

1. The best writing is often very personal. All kinds of experiences-serious, funny, unexplained, fleeting-can influence our lives and help make us who we are. Tell us about a person, place, or event in your life that has particular meaning for you, and why it is important to you. We'd especially like to hear about someone or something that has affected your life that may not have been noticed by other people.

2. Tell us about something you did last Sunday afternoon.

3. Television sitcoms often revolve around the interactions of a group of people with unique personalities. Write about your interaction with your friends. Explain why you and your friends might become the next great sitcom, and describe your role in the show.

4. Select a creative work-a novel, a film, a musical piece, a painting, or other work of art-that has influenced the way you view the world and the way you view yourself. Discuss the impact the work has had on you. (We are less interested in a detailed plot summary or a description of the work that in hearing how the work has affected you.)

D. Please write an essay (250-500 words) on a topic of your choice or on one of the options listed below.

1. Evaluate a significant experience, achievement, or risk that you have taken and its impact on you.

2. Discuss some issue of personal, local, national, or international concern and its importance to you.

3. Indicate a person who has had a significant influence on you, and describe that influence.

4. Describe a character in fiction, an historical figure, or a creative work (as in art, music, science, etc.) that has had an influence on you, and explain that influence.

Descriptive Statements

Answer the following:

a. Who or what influenced you to apply to University X?

b. What are your academic and career aspirations?

c. Describe your most meaningful activity outside the classroom.

Writing Sample

Please send us a graded writing assignment from a high school English or history class. Or, submit an essay (up to one page) on one of the following topics:

1. What experiences or circumstances have influenced your academic performance?

2. College X values a diverse student body. What contributions might you make to our campus community outside of academic achievement?

Other Application Sections

Some applications will request that you submit separate sections to capture "other than" academic information about yourself. A good way to prepare for this type of question is to construct a Resume, which includes dates and lists your work experience, extracurricular, personal and volunteer activities and academic honors. A sample resume follows on the next page and a blank Resume Template (Appendix D) is provided in the back of this Guide.

SAMPLE RESUME

Jessica D. Brown
Home Address
City, State, Zip Code
Home Phone; Cell Phone
Email address

Education
September 2010 – present
University Heights High School, Utopia, MA
92.3 GPA
2200 SAT I score; 33 ACT score
English SAT II – 85
Japanese SAT II – 78
Expected Year of Graduation: 2014

Academic Recognition
National Honor Society (member)
2011 – present
Intel Science Award
2012

Extracurricular Activities
Soccer Team
Dance Club

Work Experience
Bogle Printing Services
Summer 2011
- Cashier
Collected payment from customers

Leadership Experiences
Student Government (Secretary) 2012-2013
- Take notes at all meetings, distribute news items
Moriah Baptist Church (Youth Group Coordinator)
2012-2013
- organize programs for youth group, ages 13 to 18

Volunteer Experiences
Utopia Public Library, Utopia, MA
February – August 2012
- read to young children, ages 4 and 5 Utopia HS
College Office
January – June 2013
- answer phone calls and make copies

 TIP **Avoid use of an inappropriate email identity, i.e. "Hotlips@..."**
or Sexy13@...

Understanding

College Costs &

Financial Aid

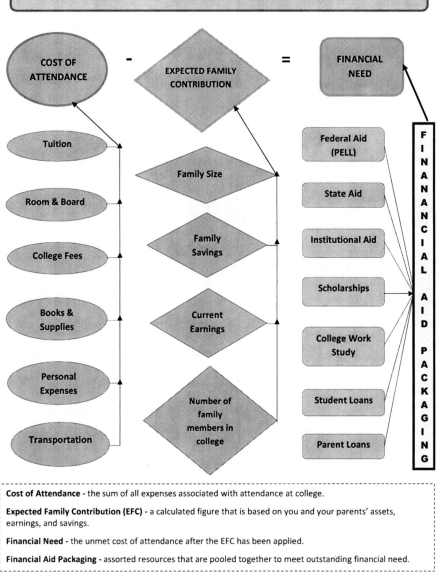

Cost of Attendance - the sum of all expenses associated with attendance at college.

Expected Family Contribution (EFC) - a calculated figure that is based on you and your parents' assets, earnings, and savings.

Financial Need - the unmet cost of attendance after the EFC has been applied.

Financial Aid Packaging - assorted resources that are pooled together to meet outstanding financial need.

FINANCIAL AID LEXICON

Award Letter – when admitted to a college, a letter is sent outlining the kind of financial aid a student is eligible for, which might include federal, state and individual college sources of assistance.

College Discovery Programs – are *educational opportunity programs* offered at the 2-year colleges within the City University of New York (CUNY).

Cost of Attendance – the sum of all expenses associated with attendance at a college. It includes the cost of tuition and fees, books and supplies, room and board, personal expenses, and transportation.

Educational Loans – financial assistance that is given to the student and/or parents that must be repaid with interest. Student loans include Federal Stafford loans (subsidized and unsubsidized), Federal Direct Loans and Federal Perkins loans. Parent loans include the Federal Parent Loans for Undergraduate Students (FPLUS) and loans offered by colleges and universities.

Educational Opportunity Programs (EOP) – targets academically and economically disadvantaged students at State University of New York (SUNY) colleges and universities.

Expected Family Contribution (EFC) – The EFC is calculated when a student and their parent's assets, earnings, and savings are submitted on a FAFSA application. When the EFC figure is deducted from the cost of attendance, the true financial need amount is identified. It is this amount that can be offset by grants, scholarships, work study and/or loans.

FAFSA (Free Application for Federal Student Aid) – a form to be completed to apply for federal financial aid. It is used to award grants and loans, such as the Pell Grant, Federal Supplemental Educational Opportunity Grant, Perkins Loan, Stafford Loan and Federal Work-Study. Important: *File FAFSA soon after January 1st of the senior year.*

Fee Waivers – students who meet certain low-income guidelines may qualify for a fee waiver to reduce or eliminate college application fees or SAT test-taking fees.

Financial Aid – any sources of financial assistance that help pay for college, i.e. grants, scholarships, educational loans, college work-study, and federal (PELL) and state assistance programs.

Federal Pell Grant – awards to students enrolled full or part-time at the undergraduate level. Eligibility for Pell is based on financial need determined by total income, net worth (excluding home and family farm equity), family size and the number of children in college.

Financial Aid Calculator – a tool to help students estimate how much financial aid they may qualify for. Many institutions have loaded "calculators" on their financial aid web pages.

Financial Aid Package – consists of assorted resources that are pooled together to address outstanding financial need. College financial aid offices will recommend using grants, scholarships, work-study and/or loans to meet the full cost of attendance at the institution.

Financial Need – the "unmet" financial amount after the expected family contribution and all scholarships and grants are deducted from the cost of attending college, for example:

$$ Cost of Attending College

- $ Expected Family Contribution (EFC)

= $ Financial Need

Federal Supplemental Educational Opportunity Grants (FSEOG) – grants awarded by colleges to Pell Grant recipients with *exceptional* financial need and can range up to $4,000 per year for undergraduate students.

Grant – a type of financial aid that does not have to be paid back.

Higher Education Opportunity Program (HEOP) – is a program for academically and economically disadvantaged New York State students. It provides financial aid to cover the majority of college costs, academic tutoring, and counseling at a number of private colleges.

Loan – money that is advanced to the student and <u>must be repaid</u> under specified conditions. A signed promissory note is required to obtain a loan.

Merit-based Assistance – any form of financial aid awarded on the basis of merit or academic achievement and not on financial need.

Military Student Aid – funds that are available to veterans and their dependents or to students who wish to enter the military.

Need-based Assistance – financial aid awarded on the basis of a student's financial need.

Part-time – attendance at college for 6-11 credits per semester and paying at a per credit rate. Overtime, it is more expensive to attend college this way.

Perkins Loan – low-interest (5%) loan for students with exceptional financial need.

PLUS Loan – parents with an acceptable credit history can borrow money (at a low variable interest rate) to help pay college expenses. Parents can borrow for the outstanding amount remaining <u>after</u> all financial aid sources have been deducted from the cost of attendance.

PROFILE – many colleges, universities, graduate and professional schools and scholarship programs use the information collected on PROFILE to help them award non-federal student aid funds. It is a program sponsored by the College Board.

Room and Board – the cost of living on-campus, which includes a room and meals.

Scholarships – funds awarded to a student, usually based on academic achievement. These monies do not have to be repaid and are provided by the college/university or through private sources.

Student Aid Report (SAR) – the SAR is sent to you, after you file a *Free Application for Federal Student Aid* (FAFSA). It will contain your *Expected Family Contribution* (EFC) and will determine the amount of federal student aid you will receive from colleges that have offered you admission.

SEEK Program (Search for Education, Elevation and Knowledge) – is an *educational opportunity program* for academically motivated students who can demonstrate significant financial need. The program is available at the 4-year colleges within the City University of New York (CUNY) and provides free tutoring, academic and career counseling, financial assistance for 10 semesters plus 2 summers, and financial aid counseling.

Stafford Loans – a "student" loan to address "unmet need" after the Expected Family Contribution (EFC) has been deducted from the cost of attendance. Note: Six (6) months after you terminate school, you will have to begin repaying the loan (whether you graduate or not).

Tuition – the cost of taking classes at a college/university, charged at a part-time or full-time rate.

Tuition Assistance Program (TAP) – a grant program for New York State residents attending a college in the State full-time. Eligibility for TAP is based on NYS net taxable income and allows you to be screened for scholarships for academic excellence and child of veteran awards.

Work Study – a form of financial aid wherein eligible students are provided paid, part-time work assignments on-campus.

Scholarship Resources

The following list is a sampling of reputable scholarships that you can investigate. Visit websites for detailed eligibility criteria and application deadline dates. You should also investigate your *State Scholarship* offerings and *Freshman Scholarships* available at the colleges of your choice.

Name of Scholarship	Website	Description
AFA Teens for Alzheimer's Awareness College Scholarship	www.afateens.org/about_new.html	HS senior can apply for 3 scholarships ranging from $250 to $5,000
AFSA Scholarship Program	www.afsascholarship.org/hsinformation.html	HS seniors can compete for 10 scholarships at $2,000 each.
American Cancer society Youth Scholarship	www.cancer.org	HS seniors who were diagnosed with cancer before the age of 21. Award amounts vary.
American Chemical Society Scholars Program	www.acs.org/scholars	High-achievers in chemistry or science from underrepresented minority groups with a 3.0 GPA. Awards are based on financial need and range from $2,500 to $5,000.
Angel on My Shoulder Scholarship	www.angelonmyshoulder.org	HS senior who is a cancer survivor can apply for $1,000 award.

ANS Incoming Freshman Scholarship (American Nuclear Society)	new.ans.org/honors/scholarships/	HS seniors wanting to pursue a degree in nuclear engineering can apply for 4 awards at $1,000.
BigSun Scholarship	http://bigsunathletics.com	HS senior athlete can apply for one award of $500.
Best Buy Scholarship Program	http://pr.bby.com/?s=scholarships	9-12th graders can apply for scholarships of $1,000 each year.
The Buick Achievers Scholarship Program	www.buickachievers.com	HS seniors can apply for awards ranging from $2,000 to $25,000.
Burger King McLamore Foundation	www.bkmclamorefoundation.org	HS seniors can apply for awards ranging from $1000 to $50,000.
Carolina/ Mahatma Rice Scholarship	http://scholarship.mahatmarice.com/	HS seniors can apply for (21) $2,000 awards
Coca-Cola Scholarships	www.coca-colascholars.org/	HS seniors can apply for 250 four-year achievement-based scholarships.
Columbus Citizens Foundation High School Scholarship Program	www.columbuscitizensfd.org/ scholarships/highschool.html	HS seniors of Italian descent and 3.0 GPA/85 average can apply.
The Gates Millennium Scholars	http://www.gmsp.org/	1,000 students are selected each year to receive "good-through-graduation" awards to use at college of student choice.
Hispanic Scholarship Fund	www.hsf.net	HS seniors to apply for awards ranging from $1,000 to $15,000.

Horatio Alger Scholarship	www.horatioalger.org/scholarships	HS senior planning to attend four-year college and have critical financial need. Monetary awards vary by state.
Jackie Robinson Scholarship Program	http://www.jackierobinson.org/apply/programs.php	Minority HS senior can apply for 4-yr scholarships up to $7,500 per year.
John F. Kennedy Profile in Courage Essay Contest	http://www.jfklibrary.org/Education	9-12th graders can compete in the contest. Awards range from $500 to $10,000.
Joseph Tauber Scholarship Program	http://1199seiubenefits.org/funds-and-services/child-care-funds/youth-programs/jts/	Children of eligible 1199 SEIU members to be considered for need-based awards, with a minimum award of $750.
KFC Colonel's Scholars Program	www.kfcscholars.org	HS seniors who intend in-state public college/university and have financial need can apply for (50) $20,000 awards
Knights of Columbus Scholarship	kofc.org/en/scholarships/index.html	Children of Knights of Columbus members can apply for awards
The Komen College Scholarship Program	http://ww5.komen.org/ResearchGrants/CollegeScholarshipAward.html	HS senior must be a breast cancer survivor or have lost a parent to breast cancer. Apply for awards of $10,000 p/yr. for four years.
Lowe's Scholarship	www.lowes.com; search "scholarships"	HS seniors can apply for (140) $2,500 awards.
The Maureen L. & Howard N. Blitman, P.E., Scholarship to Promote Diversity in Engineering	www.nspe.org/Students/Scholarships/index.html	HS seniors who are members of underrepresented minority groups and accepted to a ABET-accredited engineering program can apply for award of $5,000 for first college year.
National Multiple Sclerosis Society	www.nationalmssociety.org	HS seniors with MS, or a parent with MS, can apply for awards ranging from $1000 to $3000.

National Young Arts Foundation	www.youngarts.org	Aspiring artists in grades 10-12 can apply for program in nine (9) artistic disciplines & access to $500,000 in scholarship monies.
Prudential Spirit of Community Award	http://spirit.prudential.com	5-12 graders. State honorees receive $1,000 and National honorees receive $5,000.
Pfzier Epilepsy Scholarship	Epilepsy-scholarship.com	HS senior who has been diagnosed with epilepsy can apply for (25) $3,000 awards.
Ron Brown Scholarship	www.ronbrown.org/Home.aspx	Outstanding African-American HS seniors can apply for 10-20 annual awards of $10,000 p/yr.
SMART Scholarship (Science, Mathematics, and Research for Transformation)	http://smart.asee.org	HS seniors interested in science & engineering and willing to accept post-graduate employ at the Dept. of Defense. Apply for awards ranging from $25,000 to $38,000.
Thurgood Marshall Scholarship Fund	http://thurgoodmarshallfund.net/scholarship/about-scholarships-program	HS seniors can apply for a variety of awards sponsored by Coca-Cola, Lowe's, Costco, Ford and the National Hockey League.
United Negro College Fund (UNCF)	Uncf.org	The UNCF manages various scholarship programs, each with its own eligibility criteria. Check out website for details.
Washington Crossing Foundation	http://www.gwcf.org/SchlProgram.html	HS seniors planning careers in government service can apply for awards ranging from $500 to $5,000.

Pre-Freshman To-Do List

You've made your final college selection; now what? Here are some tips to guide your transition from high school senior to registered college freshman.

1. Read your mail thoroughly, top to bottom.

2. Organize your mail and important papers in a clearly marked filing system.

3. Get those deposits in on time! An admissions deposit or commitment fee is likely to be requested by May 1st. Also, a dormitory deposit may be requested by June.

4. Before releasing an original document, make a copy for your files.

5. Call for office hours before making a trip to the campus.

6. Always get the name of the person you do business with, on the phone and in person.

7. When visiting campus offices, be polite and use last names, e.g., Mr. Lee or Mrs. Perez.

8. Be prepared to submit your medical inoculation history along with a completed physical examination form – the college will likely provide you with forms for your family physician to complete. **Freshmen will be prevented from registering for classes until medical requirements are met.**

9. So that you will be in the best position to secure classes for your first term, it is to your advantage to register for classes *early*. In many cases, freshmen can register by the end of June.

10. Many colleges offer a pre-freshman summer program. This can be a great opportunity to sample freshman offerings and become familiar with the campus, before all students return in the fall. *With rare exceptions*, freshmen should <u>not</u> take classes for credit during the rising freshman summer, because of the rigor required. Summer courses condense what is normally taught in a 12- to 15-week semester into six weeks. And once a grade has been issued in a credit-bearing course, it <u>cannot</u> be expunged.

11. **When in doubt, ASK!** Speak directly with college representatives, who are ready and willing to assist you. For sure, you don't want to risk getting wrong information by listening to your peers.

12. Use the **Freshman Transition Form** (Appendix L) to record your progress.

Did You Know?

 Even if standardized test scores are printed on your high school transcript, colleges will want you to request official scores from the testing service.

Parent's

Corner

Message to Parent

Dear Parent,

You will probably be surprised to learn that your teenager is the main target for *Cash Poor or College? The Essential Guide to College Admissions* for *Teens (ages 13 to 18) & Their Parents.* Why, you might ask? Because I believe that most teens are completely capable of assuming *primary* responsibility for their educational performance and outcomes when they enter high school.

This is not to suggest that you have no role. To the contrary, there is much for you to do to become the effective "wind beneath your children's wings." You must champion their efforts, ensure that they are progressing properly, serve as an advocate and support lifeline throughout the teenage years, and navigate your offspring to opportunities that they cannot otherwise access on their own. Above all, you must communicate *your* interest in seeing them attend college so that they clearly understand your high expectations for them.

This is where *Cash Poor or College?* can be of real benefit to you. It provides your teen with key information and tools to support his or her college preparatory journey by:

1. Discussing the importance of continuing education beyond high school, to prepare well for the jobs of tomorrow.

2. Revealing the optimal academic preparation to ensure college access.

3. Outlining the college search process and college admissions planning phases in detail.

4. Presenting the information, on a year-by-year basis, so that it can be digested easily as your teen moves throughout high school.

5. Providing a host of practical assignments, forms, and checklists that are furnished to help your teen track his or her progress and results.

It will be enormously helpful if you can familiarize yourself with the student content portion of this book so that you, too, will be well informed and can monitor your teen's progress.

In closing, I hope that you will find this material to be helpful and in complete support of your parental dreams for your teen's advancement and success. *Good luck!*

Best wishes,

Diane M. Warmsley

Parent and Author

Ways to Support Your Teen in High School

▶ *Set expectations high.*

If there were but one thing you could do to impact your teen's future, I would urge you to set high expectations as he or she enters high school. Hopefully, that's what you have done up to this threshold, but if not, this is a fresh opportunity to do so. Children rise to the level of our expectations for them. And we need to understand that they will not break or crumble when we ask them to perform at their very best. It is remarkable to see what children can achieve when they truly put forth effort and strive to reach a goal. If you want your teen to be college-bound, then your expectations of academic performance must align with that goal and that process begins with setting the bar high.

▶ **Insist on a college prep program.**

The first order of business in setting your expectations is to require that your children pursue a program in high school that seeks to 1) prepare them to access the best colleges possible, and 2) ensure that they will be well-prepared to succeed in college, once there. The *most optimal* program that promises to deliver on both fronts is a "college preparatory program."

Your teen's progress in this program should insure that, by the end of the junior year, the following classes have been fulfilled:

3 years English

3 years Mathematics (Algebra, Geometry, Trigonometry, pre-Calculus, Calculus)

3 years Science (Biology, Chemistry, Physics, Earth/Space Science)

2-3 years of Social Studies

2-3 years of Foreign Language

1 year of performing or visual arts

Your annual meeting with a guidance counselor should encompass academic coursework for the following year that shows progress in accordance with the program. (Your teen is introduced to this academic program in the "Freshman" section of this Guide.)

▶ *Encourage math throughout high school.*

If you want your child to have access to the best colleges, then it's essential to keep math in the academic program. A 2008 report stated that "Taking higher-level math courses is key to access to postsecondary education [college], especially for disadvantaged and minority students."[9] Additional studies have shown that the more math teens take in high school, the more prepared they are for college-level work. It also follows that the more prepared a student is, the more likely he/she will be to complete a degree.

Last, strong math preparation positions students to take advantage of a wider range of college majors, such as engineering, architecture, information technology, manufacturing, and so many more. For all these reasons, I urge you to encourage strong math development in your teen.

Did You Know?

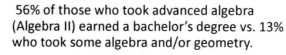

56% of those who took advanced algebra (Algebra II) earned a bachelor's degree vs. 13% who took some algebra and/or geometry.

73% of students who take calculus earned a bachelor's degree compared to 3% who took general or basic math.[10]

▶ *Accept grades of 80 or higher, only.*

Every subject is not going to be your child's best subject. But, with good study habits, just about every child can pull out *at least* a grade of 80 in each class. Set this as a *minimum* standard — the grade that your child should not fall below. If you are monitoring performance closely, you will know if your children have done their best, in which case, you can cut them some slack if they fall short. Otherwise, set the bar and keep it there!

▶ **Ask about experiences *in* and *out* of school.**

The world has become so much more complex for this generation. Therefore, it is vitally important to assess how your child is faring in the high school environment. The teen years are naturally fraught with challenges, so you'll want to be on the alert for issues that drain self-esteem and depress academic performance. Be prepared to lend support around any number of sensitive issues—bullying, peer pressure, body-image changes, dating, discrimination, "do's" and "don'ts" of proper technology use.

▶ *Encourage friendships that are uplifting.*

Over the course of the high school years, teens need to build strong self-esteem and confidence in their decision-making, and become discerning about the people in their lives. Nowhere is this more important than in their selection of friends. As a parent, you will want to monitor friendships that can do damage to the healthy development of your child. Your oversight must be handled delicately as teens have an uncanny ability to sense parental disapproval and, whether consciously or unconsciously, gravitate in the direction we don't wish them to go. Instead, it might be helpful to find ways to limit access to those who don't meet your approval, while creating opportunities to encourage relationships of value.

▶ *Help build financial literacy.*

The high school years are a great time to help a teen learn something about the value of money, as in wise spending and savings habits. This intentional learning experience is now known as "financial literacy." If you have not already done so, assist your teen with opening a savings account and encourage good saving habits, especially for college.

Next, encourage maintenance of a budget – the practice of monitoring one's personal funds will sensitize a teen to the flow of money. Practical lessons such as these will be needed when your teen gets to college, so starting early can ensure good habits down the road. A *Personal Budget Worksheet* (Appendix I) is provided to track typical teenage expenses, on a weekly basis.

▶ *Buddy-up with other parents.*

Parents need support, too! The work of raising children and helping them reach their full potential can feel like a daunting journey, especially when they enter the teen years. But if the work is shared with like-minded parents, the burden can be substantially reduced. Even working with just one other parent can be enormously helpful. You might try to share responsibilities, such as researching enrichment and summer programs, attending important forums, locating scholarships, finding resource materials, and whatever else may be relevant. *Remember, a load shared is a load cut in half!*

▶ *Encourage reading and vocabulary growth.*

The best way for a child to learn to value reading is by example. Parents simply set an example by actively reading themselves. Some parents enjoy reading the same books as their teen, so that lively discussions can ensue. Whatever the family practice, try not to restrict reading materials for your teen, unless they are absolutely inappropriate or objectionable. Remember, a true love of reading usually develops through latching onto a particular type of literature that is read for pleasure.

You can also encourage vocabulary development by finding a way to use new words. One of my favorite weekly activities was to post a new word on the refrigerator with its definition. When two or more family members were in the kitchen, each was encouraged to use the word in a sentence. At other times, just seeing the word, day after day, works to subliminally implant it. This is a great way to get your teen to painlessly prep for the SAT! Words can be downloaded at www.freevocabulary.com.

▶ *Utilize summer enrichment programs.*

Summer can be the most misused time during a teenager's journey. For years, many parents have thought that teens deserved a full two-month break from school, as a kind of reward. A nice thought! But what this really creates for young folk is a *slippage in skills*. When the fall term arrives, some students are ready to advance on day one, while others struggle to regain ground.

Instead, parents might consider the benefit of keeping young people engaged in enriching and productive activities. This does not mean that teens must forego fun! Many summer programs package enrichment with recreation activities. On the enrichment side, offerings can include exposure to a wide range of fields of study, career exploration and/or talent-based programming.

Sometimes, enrichment programs are offered right in the neighborhood at local libraries, museums, camps or on college campuses. If fees for participation are expected, be sure to inquire about financial assistance that may be available to lower or completely eliminate registration costs.

Not only do these kinds of experiences shrink the achievement gap that can take place over the summer months, but they also give students great writing material for the college and scholarship applications that they will encounter down the road.

Did you know?

 "A study from Johns Hopkins University of students in Baltimore found that...learning loss is cumulative, summer after summer. It has a tremendous impact on students' success, including high school completion, post-secondary education and work force preparedness."[11]

▶ *Encourage children to step outside of their comfort zone.*

Growing into young adulthood requires stepping up to assume new responsibilities and trying on new ideas. But some young people shrink from this developmental process, becoming anxious and fearful about confronting new experiences. This, in turn, can jeopardize their ability to adjust properly when situated in college.

To nudge a young person forward, a parent should be encouraging, supportive and, above all, avoid slipping into judgmental or overly critical responses. Always, parents must provide a safe place to fall, as teens test out new ideas and brave new experiential paths.

▶ *Expose your teen to the Arts.*

Exposure to the arts is not a frivolous venture. To the contrary, when students take classes in the arts, it unlocks their right-brain potential and invites them to explore their creative abilities. Students who engage in the arts develop an appreciation for activities that not only entertain, but also encourage a healthy release of excess energy and emotion – something teens seem to have in abundance. Whether it is music, dance, drama, or the visual arts, *all* help young folk develop strong communication skills, build self-confidence and clarify their perceptions about the world.

▶ *Be fully available senior year.*

The senior year of high school can be daunting. Not only are teens expected to complete all work associated with senior year classes, they also must keep up with the paper flow and mandatory deadlines that attend to the college admission process, as well. Even the most organized young person can become overwhelmed and unravel due to the pressure. This is where you can be of enormous help to your teen – helping to organize college materials, ensuring attendance at important events, staying on top of deadlines, and managing your teen's fears and anxieties. So, in order to provide this level of support, it is recommended that you plan to be present and available throughout the senior year. There will be plenty of time to celebrate after your child has successfully registered for their first set of freshman classes.

A Final Thought

As stated earlier, you have a vital role to play throughout your child's educational experience, including the high school years. But you are now encouraged to *lead from behind.* This would mean that your teen is held accountable for his/her school performance, while you provide support wherever needed. Your increased level of engagement is to meet with school personnel, attend school forums, provide resources, investigate opportunities, and continue to serve as an encourager, supporter, self-esteem booster, disciplinarian, and confidant. When parents and teens direct their efforts in this cooperative manner, the payoff can be wonderfully rewarding as successful college admission and completion is achieved. To provide you with the maximum level of support, here's one last tool for your *Parent Toolkit.*

Introducing A College Preparation Pledge

On the next page is a **College Preparation Pledge.** I strongly encourage you to sit down with your teen to discuss its terms. Once agreement has been reached on the importance of making this commitment, your teen should sign and date it. The original should remain with you and a copy given to your child.

Throughout the high school years, you and your teen should review the Pledge to ensure that the terms are being met. Should there be any faltering it is up to you to remind your teen of their original commitment. Getting your teen back on track, as quickly as possible, is *essential* if the long term goal of college participation and completion is to be realized.

My College Preparation Pledge

This *College Preparation Pledge* is being offered to you by your parent to support you during your high school years. This document will stand as the commitment you make to yourself, as well as to your parent(s), to execute the winning strategies laid out in *Cash Poor or College?* As you consider its terms, remember that the end goal is to ensure your successful preparation for college and beyond. <u>Please read it carefully, discuss it with your parent, sign and date it.</u> Your parent keeps the original and you keep a copy. From this point forward, you are set to work towards your highest possibilities with the vital support of those who have your best interests at heart!

I pledge to fulfill the following requirements to prepare myself for the best college admission and completion outcomes.

1. I commit to completing a *College Preparatory Program* throughout my high school years.
2. I commit to achieving the best grades that I can attain and will not accept grades that fall below 80.

3. I will make every effort to complete three years of math and foreign language.

4. I will bring material to read anytime I am likely to be waiting for long periods of time, ex. doctor's office, travel, hair/nail salon, sports events, etc.

5. I will reach out for tutoring help promptly, if I find myself struggling in a class.

6. I commit to saving money from gifts and scholarships in a College Fund, to be established as soon as possible.

7. I will cultivate positive relationships that support and lift me up.

8. I will utilize my summers productively: volunteering time and/or participating in summer programs to develop new skills and explore careers.

9. I will review *The Essential Guide to College Admissions* on a routine basis, especially during summer months, in preparation for the upcoming year in high school.

10. I will use social media wisely!

Name _____

(please print)

Signature _____

Date _____

Appendices

Appendix A

THE A, B, C's OF COLLEGE TERMS

Academic advisement – academic assistance provided to students to help plan their courses of study.

The ACT® – This test covers five skill areas: English, Mathematics, Reading, Science and an optional Writing test. Most colleges accept the submission of these exam results, in place of or in addition to the SAT I. Register online at www. actstudent.org.

ACT® Plan – is a sample test that prepares students to take the ACT Test. It includes testing in four areas: English, Mathematics, Reading, and Science.

Advanced Placement Courses – AP courses are taught at the college-level while a student is still in high school. Usually, these courses are taken in the senior year and provide an opportunity to earn college credit or advanced standing placement at over 1,400 colleges. There are 31 courses and exams, in all. *Ask your guidance counselor about this option.*

Campus – the landmass of a college/university, including its buildings and facilities.

Catalog – the most comprehensive publication about a college; sometimes it is also called a bulletin. It is usually uploaded to the college's website and contains college policies, academic programs, admission requirements, student resources, tuition and fees, special programs, and all coursework required to complete majors, and more.

College – an institution of higher learning that grants the bachelor's degree, beyond high school completion. There are over 2500 colleges in the United States.

College Academic Average (CAA) – an average that is computed for grades received in college prep courses.

College Prep Classes – classes in the high school curriculum that help the student develop strong skills in reading, writing, quantitative reasoning and critical thinking. They invariably include English, Mathematics, Science, Social Studies, and Foreign Language and sometimes the visual and performing arts.

Common Application – over 450 colleges, including traditional Ivy League institutions, support the use of a single application that can be submitted online or in print to a number of institutions. This significantly streamlines the college application process during a very busy senior year.

Community College – an institution of higher learning that grants a 2-year degree or associate's degree. There are some 1,600 two-year institutions in the United States.

Credit(s) – the point value given to courses in college. (e.g. Art 101 = 3 credits, Psychology 101 = 4 credits). A set number of credits must be completed before a degree is granted, as determined by the given institution.

Curriculum – a course of study or specialized field, i.e. English, psychology, geology, astronomy, etc.

Degree – the completion of 2-year or 4-year college coursework, certified by a diploma. (2-year programs lead to an Associate degree; 4-year programs lead to a Bachelor degree)

Doctorate – the highest degree awarded in an academic area. Typical doctoral degrees are Ph.D. (liberal arts & sciences), Ed.D. (education), D.S.W. (social work), & J.D. (law).

Dormitories (dorms) – on-campus student housing.

Early Action – Students apply early and receive a decision well in advance of the institution's regular response date.

Early Decision – Students make a commitment to a first-choice institution where, if admitted they definitely will enroll. The application deadline and decision deadline occur early.

EDU, Inc. Common Black College Application – single application to apply to 36 Historically Black Colleges and Universities.

Essay – a writing sample that is often required as part of the college and/or scholarship application process. Colleges generally provide a topic that students are requested to address in their essay submissions.

Faculty – instructors or teachers at the college or university level.

Fee Waivers – students who meet certain low-income guidelines may qualify for a fee waiver to reduce or eliminate college application fees or SAT test-taking fees.

Financial Aid – several financial sources to help pay for college, i.e. grants, scholarships, loans, federal (PELL) and state assistance programs.

Full-time study – attending school for 12 or more credits per semester, charged at a flat tuition rate.

GED – The GED (General Educational Development) test consists of five subject tests, which when passed, provide a certificate of high school equivalency. The GED is an alternate route to demonstrating high school completion for college admissions.

Grade Point Average (GPA) – a grading system used in college and universities, ex. 4.0 = A, 3.0 = B, 2.0 = C, etc.

Historically Black Colleges & Universities (HBCUs) – a collection of 100+ institutions, located mostly throughout the South, that cater to a predominantly Black student population.

Internships – valuable opportunities to gain career insights for students who accept placement in a work environment related to their area of study; assignments provide pay and/or college credit.

IVY League Colleges – designation given to eight colleges: Brown (CT), Columbia (NY), Cornell (NY), Dartmouth (NH), Harvard (MA), Princeton (NJ), University of Pennsylvania,

(PA), and Yale (CT). It is commonly thought that these colleges have the strongest reputations among institutions of higher learning.

Liberal Arts – academic disciplines, such as history, philosophy, languages, that prepare students to speak and write well and think critically. It is the best preparation for those who are interested in going into the professions (law, medicine, teaching, etc.)

Matriculation – certification by a college or university that a student is "officially" registered and working towards a degree.

Major – an area of academic concentration or specialization. (Ex. a student who wants to obtain a degree in Accounting would be considered an Accounting major).

Master's Degree – two or three years of education taken beyond the bachelor's degree.

National Achievement Scholarship Program – Black students can be screened for recognition in the National Merit Scholarship Program, as well as, the National Achievement Scholarship Program. However, only one monetary award can be awarded. Students must *take the exam in the fall term of the junior year* to qualify for recognition, be U.S. citizens or permanent residents, and complete a section of the NMSQT application to self-identify as a Black student with interest to be compete in this program.

National Hispanic Recognition Program – honors the

highest scoring Hispanic/Latino students who take the PSAT/NMSQT®. Students must *take the exam in the fall term of the junior year* for recognition, have a cumulative grade point average of 3.0 or higher, and be U.S. citizens or permanent residents. Selected students are encouraged to list this honor on their college applications.

National Merit Scholarship Program – an academic competition wherein high school students enter the National Merit Program by taking the Preliminary SAT/National Merit Scholarship Qualifying Test (PSAT/NMSQT®). Generally, students must *take the exam in the fall term of the junior year* to have their scores qualify for this completion. Students must also be U.S. citizens or permanent residents. High scorers are acknowledged as commended students, semifinalists, finalists, or winners of $2,500 monetary awards. Additionally, qualified students can compete for monetary awards and/or special recognition in the National Achievement Scholarship Program for Black students and other corporate-based scholarships.

Open Admissions – an admission policy that accepts students on the basis of high school completion *only*. For this reason, it is considered the least selective for of admission.

Part-time – attendance at school for 6-11 credits and paying a per credit rate.

Phi Beta Kappa – is the nation's oldest and most widely known academic honor society, celebrating and advocating excellence in the liberal arts and sciences. Membership is a special honor reserved for the top 10% of each college graduating class. 283 chapters reside at colleges and universities nation-wide.[12]

PSAT/NMSQT® – a standardized test that provides firsthand practice for the SAT I. When the test is taken in the fall term of the junior year, it provides a <u>one-time chance</u> to enter competition for scholarships in the *National Merit Scholarship Program, National Achievement Scholarship Program* and the *National Hispanic Recognition Program.* The PSAT is like the SAT, except there is <u>no</u> Algebra II and <u>no</u> Essay. For more information: visit <u>www.collegeboard.com</u>.

Registration – all courses in which a student is officially enrolled in a semester.

Research University – the prime mission of private and state flagship research universities is to generate research and produce graduate students.[13]

Rolling Admissions – allows students to submit applications over a period of several weeks, instead of expecting students to meet a specific deadline date. This option can seem attractive, but students should be mindful that the later they submit an application, the more likely that they may miss-out on important pre-freshman programming, i.e. orientation, advisement and priority registration activities.

Room and Board – the cost charged to live on-campus, including dormitory room & meals.

ROTC – is a college program offered at more than 1,000 colleges and universities across the United States that prepares young adults to become officers in the U.S. Military. In exchange for a paid college education and a guaranteed post-college career, cadets commit to serve in the Military after graduation.

SAT I – a test that measures verbal, mathematical reasoning and writing skills. Colleges and universities use the SAT as one indicator among many to determine student eligibility to be successful at their institution. The SAT is scored on a scale of 200-800 for each sub-test, with a maximum achievable score of 2400. For more information and registration procedures, visit www.collegeboard.com.

SAT II Subject Tests – tests that measure how much students know about a particular academic subject and how well they can apply that knowledge. Exams are one-hour in length and are mostly multiple-choice. Many colleges require or recommend one or more of the 22 Subject Tests or admission or placement. For online registration go to www. collegeboard.com.

STEM – Science, Technology, Engineering and Mathematics areas of study.

Strength of Curriculum – refers to the rigor of an academic program that a student undertakes in high school. Colleges expect that students will take the most advanced level of coursework for which they qualify, i.e. honors and advanced placement courses.

Tribal Colleges and Universities (TCUs) – there are 32 postsecondary institutions located largely in the Midwest and Southwest that foster American Indian culture, language and traditions.[14]

Tuition – the cost charged for enrolling in classes at a college/university.

Undergraduate – a student working towards a two-year or four-year degree at a college or university.

University – an institution of higher learning that awards bachelor's degrees, as well as master's degrees and doctorates.

Viewbook – a splashy marketing publication about a college. It usually focuses on the most notable features about the college, student blurbs, campus photos, a list of college majors, and admissions criteria and directions for how to apply. Most colleges have their viewbooks loaded on their website or you can request one by mail.

Appendix B

USEFUL COLLEGE SEARCH WEBSITES

www.blackexcel.org	A College Help Network for Black Students
www.campusexplorer.com	College planning and search
www.collegexpress.com	College search & financial aid information
www.collegenet.com	College search & financial aid information
www.hbcu-central.com	Historically Black Colleges & Universities
www.mycollegeguide.org	College search/visit college websites
www.ncaaclearinghouse.org	NCAA college information & eligibility requirements
www.ope.ed.gov/security	Crime statistics on colleges (Department of Education)

www.petersons.com	College search by major & financial aid information
www.privatecolleges.com	Consortium of National Private Colleges & Universities
www.todaysmilitary.com	Education support available through the military
www.uncf.org	The United Negro College Fund
www.usnews.com/rankings	US News & World Report's "Best College" rankings

TEST PREP & TEST SCHEDULING

www.actstudent.org	ACT Online Prep & ACT Test information and registration
www.collegeboard.com//testing	PSATs test registration and information
www.sat.collegeboard.org	SAT test registration and information
www.princetonreview.com	Princeton Review Test Prep

www.kaplan.com — Kaplan Test Prep

www.freevocabulary.com — 5000 Vocabulary Words to study for the SAT

FINANCIAL AID & SCHOLARSHIPS

www.blackexcel.org/200-Scholarships — Scholarships for Minorities

www.collegeboard.org — College Board's scholarship search

www.fafsa.ed.gov — Instructions for filing the Free Application for Federal Student Aid (FAFSA) on-line

www.fastweb.com — Scholarship search

www.finaid.org — College cost projector & financial aid estimate calculator

www.nationalmerit.org — Requirements for entry to *National Merit Scholarship Program* via the PSAT/ NMSQT Test

www.salliemae.com	Paying for college and loan information
www.scholarshipsonline.org	Scholarship search updated daily
www.studentaid.ed.gov	US Department of Education financial aid guidance
www.uncf.org	6,000+ scholarships
www.wiredscholar.org	Scholarship search

CAREER EXPLORATION

www.ams.org/employment/highschool.html	Mathematics
http://science.education.nih.gov/lifeworks	Science
https://www.aamc.org/students/medstudents/cim	Medicine
http://www.hrsa.gov/index.html	Allied Health Professions
http://nacme.org	Engineering
http://www.bls.gov/k12/music.htm	Music and Arts
http://www.bls.gov/k12/	Overview of a broad range of occupations (U.S. Department of Labor)

http://bls.gov/ooh/   Occupational Outlook Handbook (see what the career of your choice requires in educational completion and pays in salaries, as well as, forecasts in growth potential in the near future)

Appendix C

BIOGRAPHICAL PROFILE

PERSONAL

Your Name _____

Date of birth _____ Birthplace _____

Country <u>or</u> City & State

Name of hospital

IMMEDIATE FAMILY

Mother's name _____

Father's name _____

Sibling _____

Name	Gender	Date of birth

Sibling _____

Name	Gender	Date of birth

Sibling _____

Name   Gender   Date of birth

Sibling _____

Name   Gender   Date of birth

Sibling _____

Name   Gender   Date of birth

RELIGION

If religion has a special place in your life, name the denomination here and indicate any special memories of your church experiences:

_____

_____

_____

PLACES OF RESIDENCE

Places where you lived:

_____

Address (if known)   City   State   How long

_____

Address (if known)   City   State   How long

_____

| Address (if known) | City | State | How long |

_____

| Address (if known) | City | State | How long |

EDUCATION

Elementary school(s) attended _____

_____

Middle school(s) attended_____

_____

High school(s) attended_____

_____

WORK EXPERIENCES

List all paid jobs you have held:

1._____

      Type of job   **Job title**   **When?**

___

2._____

     Type of job   **Job title**   **When?**

3._____

     Type of job   **Job title**   **When?**

4._____

     Type of job   **Job title**   **When?**

5._____

     Type of job   **Job title**   **When?**

List all volunteer experiences:

1._____

     Nature of experience   **Job title**   **When?**

2._____

     Nature of experience   **Job title**   **When?**

3._____

     Nature of experience   **Job title**   **When?**

4._____

Nature of experience   Job title   When?

5._____

Nature of experience   Job title   When?

List all extracurricular activities you have participated in:

1._____

Name activity   How long?

2._____

Name activity   How long?

3._____

Name activity   How long?

4._____

Name activity   How long?

5._____

Name activity   How long?

EARLY CHILDHOOD MEMORIES (birth to age 5)

Did you have a nickname and, if so, what was it?

_____

What was your favorite book(s)?

_____

What was your favorite TV show(s)?

_____

Did you have a pet(s)? _

_____

What childhood illnesses did you have?

_____

Did you attend pre-school?   [   ] Yes   [   ] No

What were the names of your best friends?

_____

Interesting places you traveled?

_____

What do you remember most about your early years?

_____

_____

_____

_____

_____

_____

CHILDHOOD RECOLLECTIONS (5 to 12 years old)

Did you have a nickname and, if so, what was it?

[   ] Yes_____ [   ] No

What were the "hot" toys and popular games you played?

_____

_____

What were your favorite foods to eat?

_____

What was your favorite color?

_____

What was your favorite books?

_____

What was your favorite movie?

_____

What were your favorite TV shows?

_____

_____

_____

What was your favorite song/music?

_____

Did you have a pet(s)?

_____

What illnesses did you have?

_____

What was your favorite subject in elementary school?

_____

In what sports/physical activity did you participate?

_____

Did you learn to play a musical instrument?

[   ] Yes _____ [   ] No

If so, what type of music did you like to play?

_____

Did you excel in a sport or other learned activity? If so, describe:

_____

_____

_____

_____

_____

_____

Who was your favorite teacher and why?

_____

_____

_____

_____

What were the names of your best friends?

_____

_____

Interesting places you traveled?

_____

_____

_____

How the family celebrated holidays or special events:

_____

_____

_____

_____

_____

What do you remember most about these years?

_____

_____

_____

_____

_____

_____

_____

_____

RECOLLECTIONS OF ADOLESCENCE (13 to Present)

Do you have a nickname and, if so, what was it?

_____

What are your favorite hobbies?

_____

What is your favorite book?

_____

What is your favorite movie?

_____

What are your favorite TV shows?

_____

What is your favorite song/music?

_____

What unusual illnesses did you have?

_____

What is your favorite subject in school?

_____

In what sports/physical activity do you participate?

_____

Do you play a musical instrument?

_____

Do you excel in a sport or other learned activity?
If so, describe

_____

_____

_____

_____

_____

Who is your favorite teacher and why?

_____

_____

_____

Are you very social?

_____

_____

_____

Interesting places you have traveled?

_____

_____

_____

What do you remember most about your high school years?

_____

_____

_____

Appendix D

RESUME TEMPLATE

Your Name

Home Address

City, State, Zip Code

Home Phone; Cell Phone

Email address

Education

Start date – present   Name of High School,

City, State _____

GPA _____

SAT I score _____; ACT score _____

SAT II subject & grade _____

SAT II subject & grade _____

Expected Year of Graduation: _____

Academic Recognition

List all honors, awards and special recognition items with associated dates

_____

_____

_____

Extracurricular Activities   Clubs, teams, church and
community activities

_____

_____

_____

Work Experience   Name of Employer

Address

Dates of employment

Description of duties

_____

_____

_____

Leadership Experiences   List all positions held in
organizations

_____

_____

_____

Volunteer Experiences   List all places where one has
volunteered and describe
nature of service

_____

_____

_____

Appendix E
PERSONAL BUDGET WORKSHEET

Weekly Budget Accounting

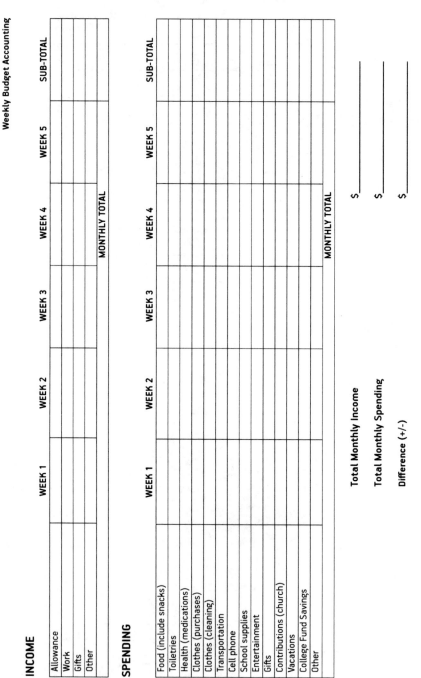

INCOME

	WEEK 1	WEEK 2	WEEK 3	WEEK 4	WEEK 5	SUB-TOTAL
Allowance						
Work						
Gifts						
Other						
				MONTHLY TOTAL		

SPENDING

	WEEK 1	WEEK 2	WEEK 3	WEEK 4	WEEK 5	SUB-TOTAL
Food (include snacks)						
Toiletries						
Health (medications)						
Clothes (purchases)						
Clothes (cleaning)						
Transportation						
Cell phone						
School supplies						
Entertainment						
Gifts						
Contributions (church)						
Vacations						
College Fund Savings						
Other						
				MONTHLY TOTAL		

Total Monthly Income $ _____

Total Monthly Spending $ _____

Difference (+/-) $ _____

Appendix F
SCHEDULING COLLEGE VISITS

Instructions: Use this form to schedule campus visits; duplicate as needed.

NAME OF COLLEGE	Open Houses			Tours				Information Sessions			Visited
	Day/Date	Day/Date	Day/Date	Day/Date	Day/Date	Day/Date	Day/Date	Day/Date	Day/Date	Day/Date	Yes/No
Address:											
	Day/Date	Day/Date	Day/Date	Day/Date	Day/Date	Day/Date	Day/Date	Day/Date	Day/Date	Day/Date	Yes/No
Address:											
	Day/Date	Day/Date	Day/Date	Day/Date	Day/Date	Day/Date	Day/Date	Day/Date	Day/Date	Day/Date	Yes/No
Address:											
	Day/Date	Day/Date	Day/Date	Day/Date	Day/Date	Day/Date	Day/Date	Day/Date	Day/Date	Day/Date	Yes/No
Address:											
	Day/Date	Day/Date	Day/Date	Day/Date	Day/Date	Day/Date	Day/Date	Day/Date	Day/Date	Day/Date	Yes/No
Address:											
	Day/Date	Day/Date	Day/Date	Day/Date	Day/Date	Day/Date	Day/Date	Day/Date	Day/Date	Day/Date	Yes/No
Address:											
	Day/Date	Day/Date	Day/Date	Day/Date	Day/Date	Day/Date	Day/Date	Day/Date	Day/Date	Day/Date	Yes/No
Address:											
	Day/Date	Day/Date	Day/Date	Day/Date	Day/Date	Day/Date	Day/Date	Day/Date	Day/Date	Day/Date	Yes/No
Address:											

Appendix G
CAMPUS VISIT QUESTIONS

Instructions: Take this form with you on college visitations and select questions to ask of Admissions Office representatives and others.

NAME OF COLLEGE _____   Date of Visit _____

| Type of Institution | [ ] 2 yr. | [ ] 4-Yr. | [ ] Public | [ ] Private | [ ] Ivy League |
| Setting | [ ] Rural | [ ] Suburban | [ ] Urban | | |

QUESTIONS	NOTES

General

What is the size of the undergraduate population?

What is the student/faculty ratio?

What is the tuition rate?

How safe is the campus?

How safe are the dorms?

Are dorms guaranteed for freshmen?

Has the college lost any program accreditations?

Admission Requirements

What HS average and SAT/ACT scores are required?

Are SAT II scores required? How many?

What are the mean SAT scores for last year's freshmen?

How many letters of recommendation are required?

Is a portfolio, audition or interview required?

Is early decision or early action available?

If the college has an Honors College, what are the criteria for entry?

Scholarships/Financial Aid

Does the college offer merit-based scholarships for freshmen?

Is need-based aid available? In what form?

Academic

What academic programs is the college best known for?

Does the college offer YOUR major of interest?

How "intense" is the academic environment for students?

What study abroad opportunities exist?

How early can students engage in research supervised by faculty?

What combined programs are offered, i.e. BA/MA?

What honors programs are available to students?

Faculty

Percentage of classes taught by tenured faculty?

Who are the college's academic "stars"?

Campus Services

Is there a mandatory system for freshmen advisement?

Does the college offer internships?

Job placement rate after graduation, by 6 months?

Services for seniors with grad school prep and job placement?

Does college have an office for students w/special needs?

Career development opportunities?

Diversity

How is the campus climate for students-of-color?

Have there been any group insensitivity issues on campus in the last 3 years? How was this handled by administration?

Do students tend to co-mingle or group together?

Does the college have a Diversity Office?

Extracurricular Activities

What opportunities exist for social activity, i.e. clubs, sororities/fraternities, community service, etc.?

What athletic programs are available?

What cultural events take place on-campus?

Follow-up Visits

What opportunities exist to sit-in on classes, spend the night in a dorm, or speak with a currently enrolled student or alumnus?

Observations (what do you see, how do you feel?)

Is college situated in an urban, suburban or rural setting?

What percentage of the population looks like you?

Do cross-cultural/racial/ethnic groups appear to mingle?

How do the dorms look, especially the rooms?

Do the campus grounds appear well-kept?

Do the cafeterias seem adequate? Taste the food?

Can you purchase a meal plan?

Other?

Appendix H
COLLEGE DATA CHART

COLLEGE NAME	Required GPA	Minimum ACT	Minimum SAT	Public/ Private	Location	2 Yr.	4 Yr.	Dorms (Y/N)	Tuition	Application Fee	App. Deadline Date

Appendix I
SCHOLARSHIP TRACKING FORM

Instructions: Use the chart below to keep track of your scholarship outreach and results. Duplicate as needed.

No.	SCHOLARSHIP NAME	Deadline Date	REQUIREMENTS				Applied Yes / No	Date Sent	Results
			Transcript	Essay	Recommendations	Other			

APPENDIX J

STUDENT ACTIVITY FORM

Complete this form and give a copy to anyone you ask for a letter of recommendation.

Student Name _____

Intended Major _____

Career Goals _____

_____

Extracurricular Activities (list all):

_____

_____

Awards, Honors, Special Recognition (list all):

_____

_____

_____

Identify any positive or negative situations that affected you during high school.

_____

_____

_____

_____

Name 3 personality traits that you like most about yourself?

_____

College Applications (list all):

1._____

2._____

3._____

4._____

5._____

6._____

7._____

8._____

9._____

10._____

Appendix K
COLLEGE ACCEPTANCE FORM

Instructions: Use this form to track your college and scholarship outcomes.

College Name/Program	Accepted ( )	Wait Listed ( )	Declined ( )	Scholarship ( )	Scholarship Amount	Deadline Date for response	Special Program Dates	Final Choice

Appendix L
FRESHMAN TRANSITION FORM

COLLEGE CHOICE _____

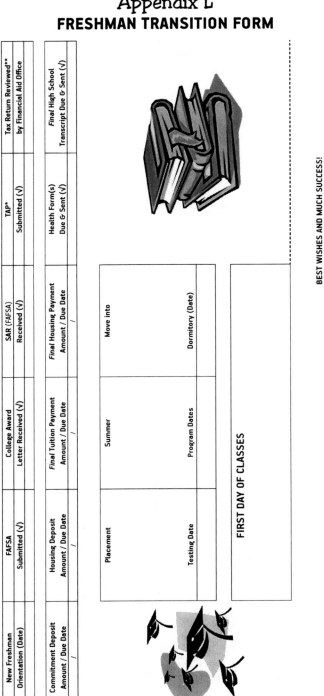

New Freshman Orientation (Date)	FAFSA Submitted (√)	College Award Letter Received (√)	SAR (FAFSA) Received (√)	TAP* Submitted (√)	Tax Return Reviewed** by Financial Aid Office
	/				

Commitment Deposit Amount / Due Date	Housing Deposit Amount / Due Date	Final Tuition Payment Amount / Due Date	Final Housing Payment Amount / Due Date	Health Form(s) Due & Sent (√)	Final High School Transcript Due & Sent (√)
/	/	/	/		

Placement	Summer	Move Into
Testing Date	Program Dates	Dormitory (Date)

FIRST DAY OF CLASSES

BEST WISHES AND MUCH SUCCESS!

* Only required if attending a college or university in New York State.
** Required if applying for an educational opportunity program.

Notes

Is College In Your Future?

1. Rahul Chowdhury, "Evolution of Mobile Phones: 1995 –2012," *Hongkiat.com,* accessed April 2012, http://www. hongkiat.com/blog/evolution-of-mobile-phones/.

2. John Baker, "Industrial Age Education is a Disservice to Students," *Huff Post Politics* (blog), March 28, 2013, http://www.huffingtonpost.com/john-baker/industrial-age-education-_b_2974297.html.

Freshmen (8ᵀᴴ and 9ᵀᴴ Grades)

3. Leo Widrich, "How the People Around You Affect Personal Success," *Lifehacker,* July 16, 2012, http://lifehacker.com/5926309/how-the-people-around-you-affect-personal-success.html.

4. John Engler, "STEM Education is the Key to the U.S.'s Economic Future," *U.S. News & World Report,* June 15, 2012, http://www.usnews.com/opinion/articles/2012/06/15/stem-education-is-the-key-to-the-uss-economic-future.html.

SOPHOMORES (10ᵀᴴ GRADE)

5. Rob Muller and Alix Beatty, "The Building Blocks of Success: Higher-Level Math for All Students," *Achieve*, May 1, 2008, www.achieve.org/files/BuildingBlocksofSuccess.pdf.

6. "ROTC Programs," *Today's Military*, http://www.todaysmilitary.com/before-serving-in-the-military/rotc-programs; "Reserve Officers' Training Corps," *Wikipedia*, last modified August 31, 2013, http://en.wikipedia.org/wiki/Reserve_Officers'_Training_Corps.

7. "Divisions," NCAA Eligibility Center, http://web1.ncaa.org/ECWR2/NCAA_EMS/NCAA_EMS.html#/; "About the NCAA," National Collegiate Athletic Association, http://www.ncaa.org/wps/wcm/connect/public/NCAA/About+the+NCAA/Membership+NEW : Membership.

8. Melissa E. Clinedinst, Sarah F. Hurley, and David A. Hawkins, *State of College Admission,* (Arlington: NACAC, 2013), 21, http://www.nacacnet.org/research/PublicationsResources /Marketplace/research/Pages/StateofCollegeAdmission.aspx.

PARENTS CORNER

9. Muller and Beatty, "The Building Blocks of Success," www.achieve.org/files/BuildingBlocksofSuccess.pdf.

10. Ibid., 6.

11. Jeff Smink, "This is Your Brain on Summer," *The New York Times,* July 27 2011, The Opinion Pages, http://www.nytimes.com/2011/07/28/opinion/28smink.html. All rights reserved. Used by permission and protected by the Copyright Laws of the United States. The printing, copying, redistribution, or retransmission of this Content without express written permission is prohibited.

THE A, B, C's OF COLLEGE TERMS

12. "The Nation's Oldest and Most Widely Known Academic Honor Society," *The Phi Beta Kappa Society,* About Us, http://www.pbk.org/infoview/PBK_InfoView.aspx?t=&id=8.

13. Lynn O'Shaughnessy, "What is a Research University," *The College Solution* (blog), May 6, 2011, http://www.thecollegesolution.com/whats-a-research-university/.

14. "White House Initiative on American Indian and Alaska Native Education," *Department of Education,* Tribal Colleges and Universities, http://www.ed.gov/edblogs/whiaiane/tribes-tcus/tribal-colleges-and-universities/.

Selected Bibliography

Baker, John. "Industrial Age Education is a Disservice to Students." *Huff Post Politics, The Blog,* 2013. http://www.huffingtonpost.com/john-baker/industrial-age-education-b_2974297.html.

Chowdhury, Rahul. "Evolution of Mobile Phones: 1995 –2012." *Hongkiat.com* (2012).

Clinedinst, Melissa E., Sarah F. Hurley, and David A. Hawkins. *State of College Admission.* Arlington: NACAC, 2013.

Engler, John. STEM Education is the Key to the U.S.'s Economic Future." *U.S. News & World Report* (15 June 2012).

Grove, Allen. "Why Does Phi Beta Kappa Matter?" *About.com.* http://collegeapps.about.com/od/choosingacollege/tp/Why-PBK-Matters.htm.

Muller and Beatty. "Achieve Policy Brief: The Building Blocks of Success: Higher-Level Math for All Students." 2008. www.achieve.org/files/BuildingBlocksofSuccess.pdf.

"Occupational Outlook Handbook." *United States Department of Labor*, Bureau of Labor Statistics. http://bls.gov/ooh.

O'Shaughnessy, Lynn. "What is a Research University," *The College Solution* (May 6, 2011).

Pirner, Karla. ""Colleges and Universities Serving Underrepresented Students." *NACAC*. 2012. http://www.nacacnet.org /college-fairs/students-parents/Documents/CollegeServingUnderserved.pdf.

Smink, Jeff. "This is Your Brain on Summer." *The New York Times* (July 27 2011).

Sullivan, Dr. Sean. *The Mind Master*. 2012. http://themindmaster.com/new/summary-scientific-basis-and-excerpt.

"The Campus Safety and Security Data Analysis Cutting Tool." *U.S. Department of Education*, Office of Postsecondary Education. http://www.ope.ed.gov/security.

"The Nation's Oldest and Most Widely Known Academic Honor Society." *The Phi Beta Kappa Society*. www.pbk.org/trademark.htm.

Widrich, Leo. "How the People Around You Affect Personal Success." *Lifehacker,* 2012. http://lifehacker.com/5926309/how-the-people-around-you-affect-personal-success.

Recommended Reading

TEENS

GENERAL

Canfield, Jack, Mark Victor Hansen, Amy Newmark, and Madeline Clapps. *Chicken Soup for the Soul: Teens Talk High School. Cos Cob:* Chicken Soup for the Soul Pub., 2008.

Carlson, Richard. *Don't Sweat the Small Stuff for Teens: Simple Ways to Keep Your Cool in Stressful Times.* New York: Hyperion, 2000.

Christen, Carol, and Richard N. Bolles. *What Color Is Your Parachute? for Teens: Discovering Yourself, Defining Your Future.* 2nd ed. Berkeley: Ten Speed Press, 2010.

Covey, Sean. *The 7 Habits of Highly Effective Teens: The Ultimate Teenage Success Guide.* London: Simon & Schuster, 2004.

The 6 Most Important Decisions You'll Ever Make: A Guide for Teens. New York: Fireside, 2006.

Galbraith M. A., Judy, and Jim Delisle. The Gifted Teen Survival Guide: Smart, Sharp, and Ready for (Almost) Anything. Minneapolis: Free Spirit Publishing, 2011.

Lawrience, Michael, Robin Jones, and Tomas Del Amo. *Self-Esteem: A Teen's Guide for Girls*. Lawrience Publishing, 2012.

Lewis, Barbara A. *What Do You Stand For? For Teens: A Guide for Building Character*. Minneapolis: Free Spirit Publishing, 2005.

Schab, Lisa M. *The Self-Esteem Workbook for Teens: Activities to Help You Build Confidence and Achieve Your Goals*. Oakland: New Harbinger Publishers, Inc., 2013.

Schwartz, Lesley. *Where's My Stuff?: The Ultimate Teen Organizing Guide*. San Francisco: Zest Books, 2007.

Senning, Cindy Post, Peggy Post and Sharon Watts. *Teen Manners: From Malls to Meals to Messaging and Beyond*. New York: Collins Pub., 2007.

Woodcock, Susan Kruger. *SOAR Study Skills: A Simple and Efficient System for Earning Better Grades in Less Time*. Grand Lighthouse Publishers, 2007.

PAYING FOR COLLEGE, FINANCIAL AID & SCHOLARSHIPS

Berntzen, Katherine. *In Pursuit of My Success for Teens: Developing a College, Career, and Money Plan for Life. 2nd ed.* Katherine Berntzen, 2011.

Brooks, Yvonne. *Financial Planning for Teens: Teen Success Series, Volume 1.* iUniverse, Incorporated, 2002.

Chany, Kalman A., and Geoff Martz. *Paying for College Without Going Broke.* New York: Random House, 2012.

Foote, Tracy. *How You Can Maximize Student Aid: Strategies for the FAFSA and the Expected Family Contribution (EFC) To Increase Financial Aid for College.* Tracy Trends, 2011.

Garfield, Patricia Saunders, and Alyson Amy Edge. *Time Worth Spending: The Top 10 Talks to Have with Your Teenager about Money.* CreateSpace Independent Publishing Platform, 2012.

Hurley, Joseph F. *The Best Way to Save for College - A Complete Guide to 529 Plans.* Savingforcollege.com, Llc, 2013.

Karchut, Wesley, and Darby Karchut. *Money and Teens: Savvy Money Money Skills.* Colorado Springs: Copper Square Studios, LLC, 2012.

O'Shaughnessy, Lynn. *The College Solution: A Guide for Everyone Looking for the Right School at the Right Price.* 2nd ed. Upper Saddle River: FT Press, 2012.

Stack, Carol, and Ruth Vedvik. *The Financial Aid Handbook: Getting the Education You Want for the Price You Can Afford.* Pequannock: Career Press, Inc., 2011.

Semagand, Geoffrey. Action Wealth Guide to Financial Literacy for Teens and Their Parents: *How to Make, Manage, Multiply and Protect Your Money.* CreateSpace Independent Publishing Platform, 2013.

Tamsen Butler, Darlene. *The Complete Guide to Personal Finance: For Teenagers.* Ocala: Atlantic Publishing Group Inc., 2010.

Tanabe, Gen, and Kelly Tanabe. *Sallie Mae How to Pay for College: A Practical Guide for Families.* Supercollege, Llc, 2011.

The Ultimate Scholarship Book 2013: Billions of Dollars in Scholarships, Grants and Prizes. Belmont: Supercollege, Llc, 2012.

1001 Ways to Pay for College: Strategies to Maximize Financial Aid, Scholarships and Grants. 6th ed. Supercollege, Llc, 2013.

The College Board. *Getting Financial Aid 2013.* College Board, 2012.

SUMMER PROGRAMS

Berger, Sandra. *Best Summer Programs for Teens: America's Top Classes, Camps, and Courses for College-Bound Students.* Chicago: Sourcebooks, Inc., 2013.

Berger, Sandra L. *The Ultimate Guide to Summer Opportunities for Teens.* Waco: Prufock Press, 2008.

Seltzer, Neill. *The 500 Best Ways for Teens to Spend the Summer: Learn About Programs for College Bound High School Students.* New York: Random House, 2004.

WRITING ESSAYS FOR COLLEGE

Barash, Carol. *Write Out Loud: Use the Story To College Method, Write Great Application*

Essays, and Get into Your Top Choice College. New York: McGraw-Hill Professional Publishing, 2013.

Bauld, Harry. *On Writing the College Application Essay: The Key to Acceptance at the College of Your Choice.* Rev. ed. New York: Collins Reference, 2012.

Hernandez, Michele. *Acing the College Application: How to Maximize Your Chances for Admission to the College of Your Choice.* New York: Ballantine Books, 2007.

Kasbar, Brian, Brian Kasbar, and Emily Angel Baer. *Essays That Worked for College Applications: 50 Essays that Helped Students Get into the Nation's Top Colleges.* Random House Publishing Group, 2003.

Tanabe, Gen and Kelly Tanabe. *50 Successful Ivy League Application Essays.* Supercollege, Llc, 2012.

PARENTS

Donati, Elisabeth. *The Ultimate Allowance.* Creative Wealth Intl., LLC, 2008.

Hudson, Chris. *Raising Resilient Teenagers: A Parent's Guide to Teenage Self-Esteem & Resilience.* Australia: Charisbel, 2012.

Roadruck, Jeremy. Your Best Child Ever: Is This Game Worth Winning? How to Raise a Stable Centered Respectful Self-Disciplined Confident.... Kindle Edition. RoadWork Publishers, Inc., 2012.

Twenge, Jean M., and W. Keith Campbell. *The Narcissism Epidemic: Living in the Age of Entitlement.* New York: Free Press, 2009.

Kunjufu, Jawanza Dr. *Raising Black Boys.* African American Images, 2007.

Butler-Derge, Shirley R. *Rites of Passage: A Program for High School African American Males.* Lanham: University Press of America, 2009.

Index